THE KOOKY 3D kids' COOKBOOK

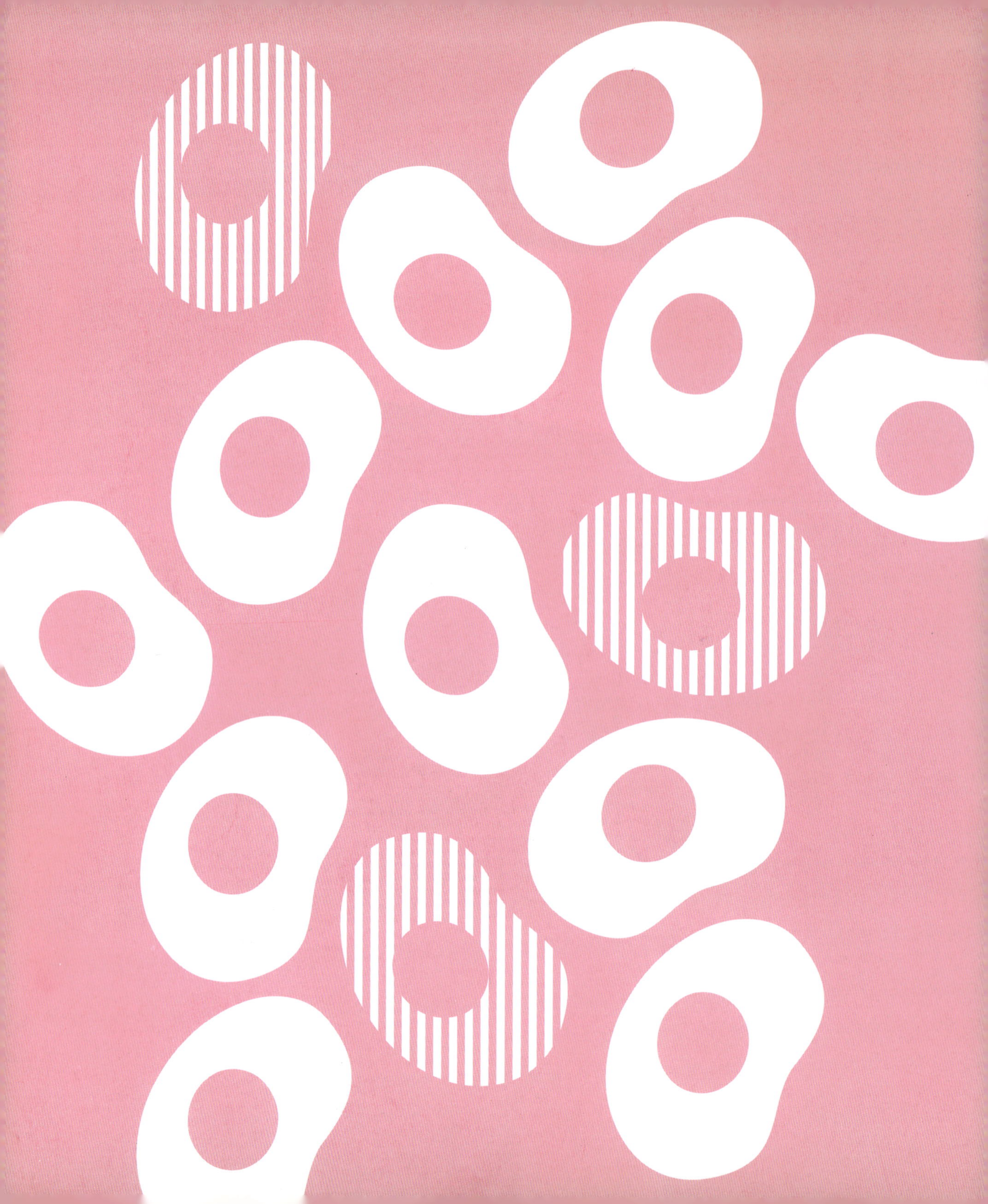

THE KOOKY 3D kids' COOKBOOK

hardie grant books
MELBOURNE · LONDON

CONTENTS

nibbles 8

BUFFALO CHICKEN WINGS / CHEESY POPCORN
PIZZETTES / DINO PASTIES
BEEFY PIES / CORN FRITTERS
MONEYBAGS / SAN CHOY BAU

big bites 26

CRUNCHY CHICKEN FINGERS / LAMB AND VEGIE KEBABS
BEAN TACOS / CHICKEN COLESLAW BURGERS
PASTA WITH MEATBALLS / VEGIE AND NOODLE STIR-FRY
CRISPY FISH NIBBLES / CHUNKY SOUP

sweets 44

CUPCAKES / MERINGUE NESTS
PIKELET STACKS / CHUNKY SPOTTY COOKIES
LAYERED JELLIES / SHAGGY LAMINGTON BLOCKS
SHORTBREAD PEOPLE / SUPERSTAR SUNDAES

Are you tired of boring 2D food? Then put on your 3D glasses and watch food come to life!

READ THIS FIRST

Cooking 3D food is not that different to cooking 2D food: you still need to follow some basic kitchen rules. Before you begin, remember to take your 3D glasses off before cooking (no wearing them while you're chopping, using equipment or going near the stovetop!). Always ask a grown-up before you start cooking (you don't want to give them a shock when they see the mess!). Ask for help if you need to do anything tricky like chopping, handling hot pans or taking things out of the oven.

Now that we've got the safety tips out of the way, next on the list is hygiene! Wash your hands with soap before you start and try to keep your work area tidy. Keep all meat in the fridge before cooking. When you've chopped raw meat, don't use the same knife and board for other ingredients that are served uncooked, such as salad leaves or fruit.

Read the recipe ALL THE WAY TO THE END before you start cooking. You might discover ingredients or equipment you don't have (and it can be really annoying if you have to pay your younger brother or sister to run to the shop).

All the spoon measures and cup measures are LEVEL so don't use more than the recipe tells you to.

If you're using the oven, arrange the shelves before you preheat the oven. A fan-forced oven will be hotter than a normal oven and doesn't need preheating. You'll need to turn your fan-forced oven 10°C (50°F) lower than the temperature in the recipe. Get a grown-up to help you with this.

When you've finished cooking, take a good look, then put on your 3D glasses and compare your dish to the picture. Magic!

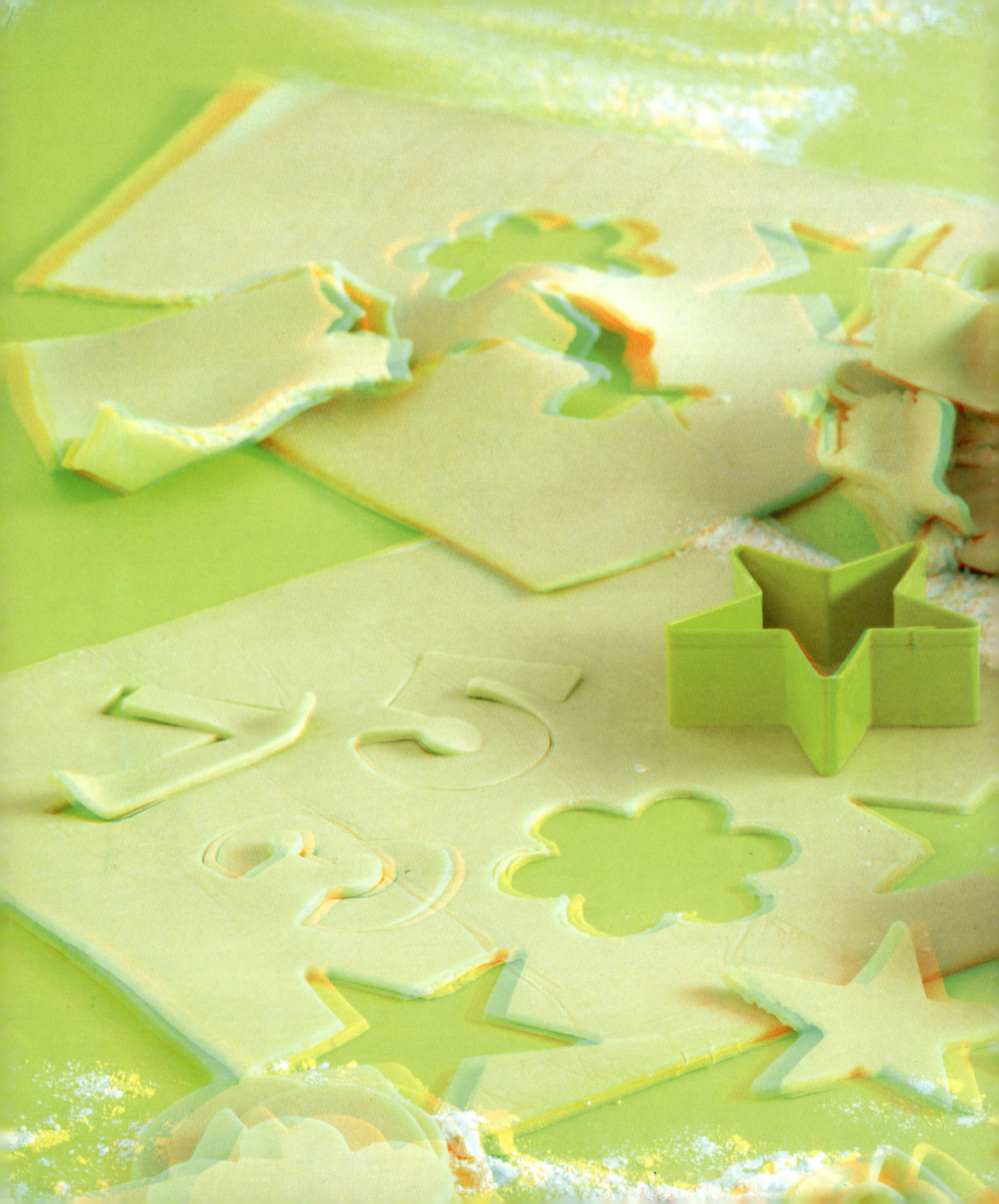

NIBBLES

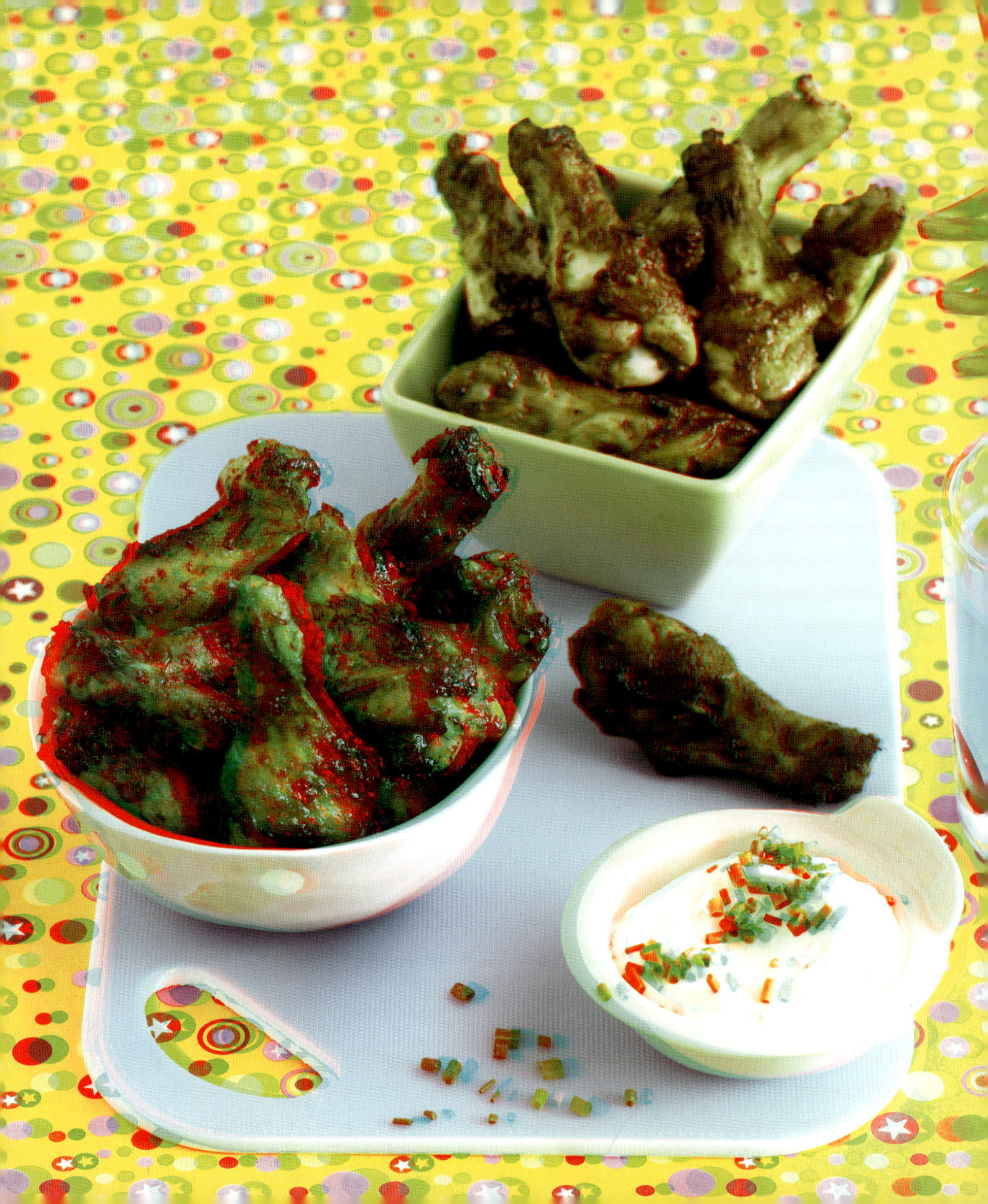

BUFFALO CHICKEN WINGS
with creamy dip

MAKES 16 | **PREP TIME** 10 MINS + MARINATING | **COOKING TIME** 20 MINS

125 ml (4 fl oz/½ cup) **tomato sauce** (ketchup)
2 **garlic cloves**, crushed
2 tablespoons **soft brown sugar**
1 tablespoon **worcestershire sauce**
1 tablespoon **olive oil**
16 **chicken** drumettes

CREAMY DIP
3 tablespoons **sour cream**
3 tablespoons **whole-egg mayonnaise**
2 tablespoons roughly chopped **chives**

1. Combine the tomato sauce, garlic, sugar, worcestershire sauce and oil in a small bowl. Put the drumettes into a shallow glass or ceramic dish. Add the sauce mixture to the chicken and toss, making sure all the pieces are coated. Cover with plastic wrap and put in the fridge for 30 minutes.

2. Preheat the oven to 200°C (400°F/Gas 6) and line a large baking tray with baking paper. Lay the drumettes out in a single layer on the tray. Bake for 20 minutes, or until the drumettes are brown and cooked through. Serve warm or cold with the dip.

3. To make the dip, mix all the ingredients in a small bowl. Keep in the fridge until ready to serve with the drumettes.

Drumettes are a section of chicken wings which are like mini drumsticks. You can also find 'wingettes', a different part of the wing, in some shops. Sometimes they are called 'chicken nibbles'. Use whichever you like.

CHEESY popcorn

MAKES ABOUT 6 CUPS | **PREP TIME** 10 MINS | **COOKING TIME** 3–4 MINS

2 tablespoons **vegetable oil**
70 g (2½ oz/⅓ cup) **popping corn**
40 g (1½ oz) **butter**, melted
1 teaspoon **Mexican chilli powder**
2 teaspoons **dried chives**
35 g (1¼ oz/⅓ cup) finely grated **parmesan cheese**

1 Heat the oil in a large saucepan over medium heat. Add the popping corn and cover tightly with a lid. Cook for 3–4 minutes, or until the popping sounds have slowed down and almost stopped.

2 Remove from the heat and drizzle the melted butter over the popcorn. Quickly sprinkle with the chilli powder, chives and parmesan.

3 Use a large metal spoon to stir the flavourings through the popcorn. Pour into a large bowl and let it cool a little before serving. This is best eaten within about 1 hour.

Make sure you use Mexican chilli powder, which is a lot less hot than ground chillies.

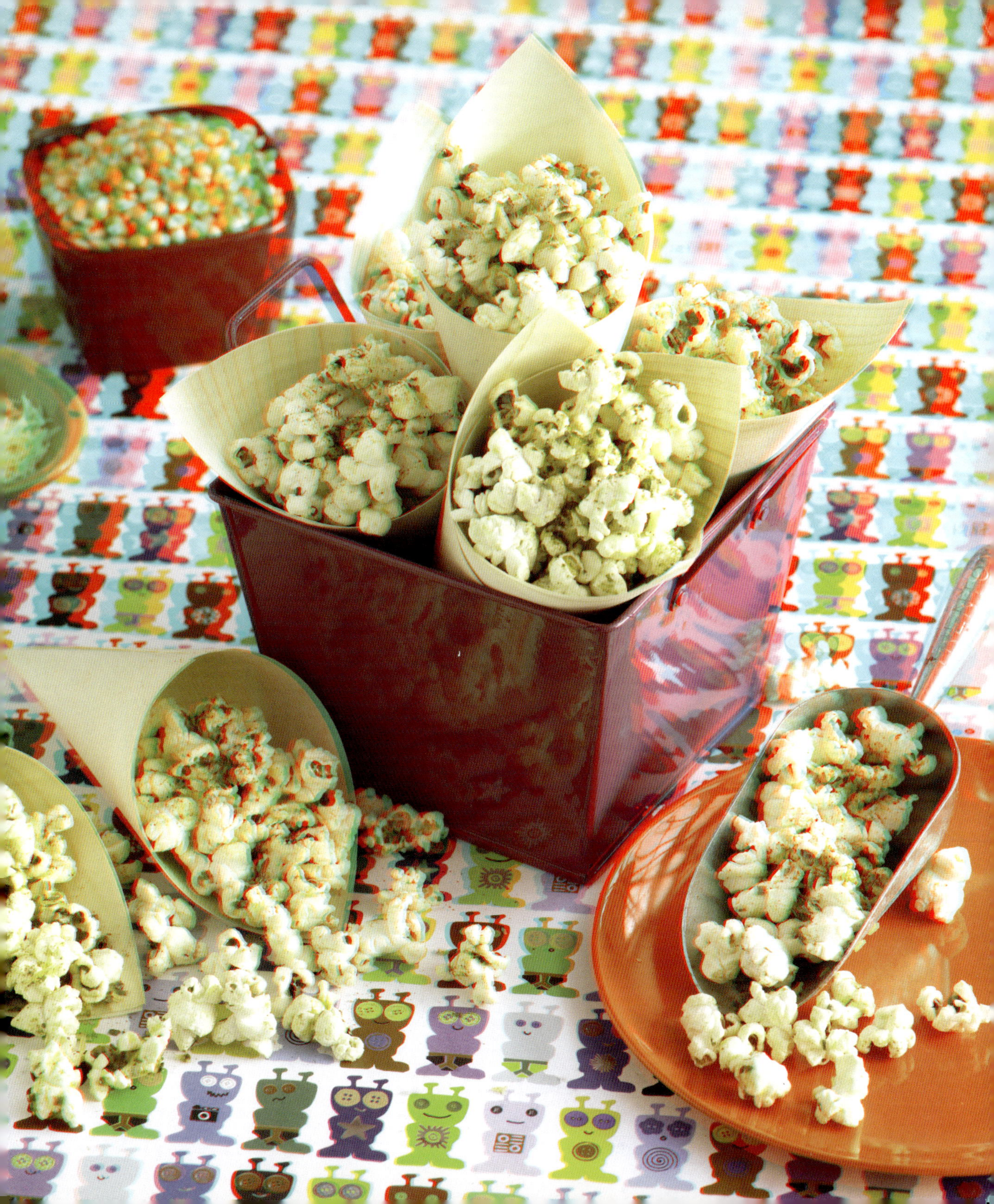

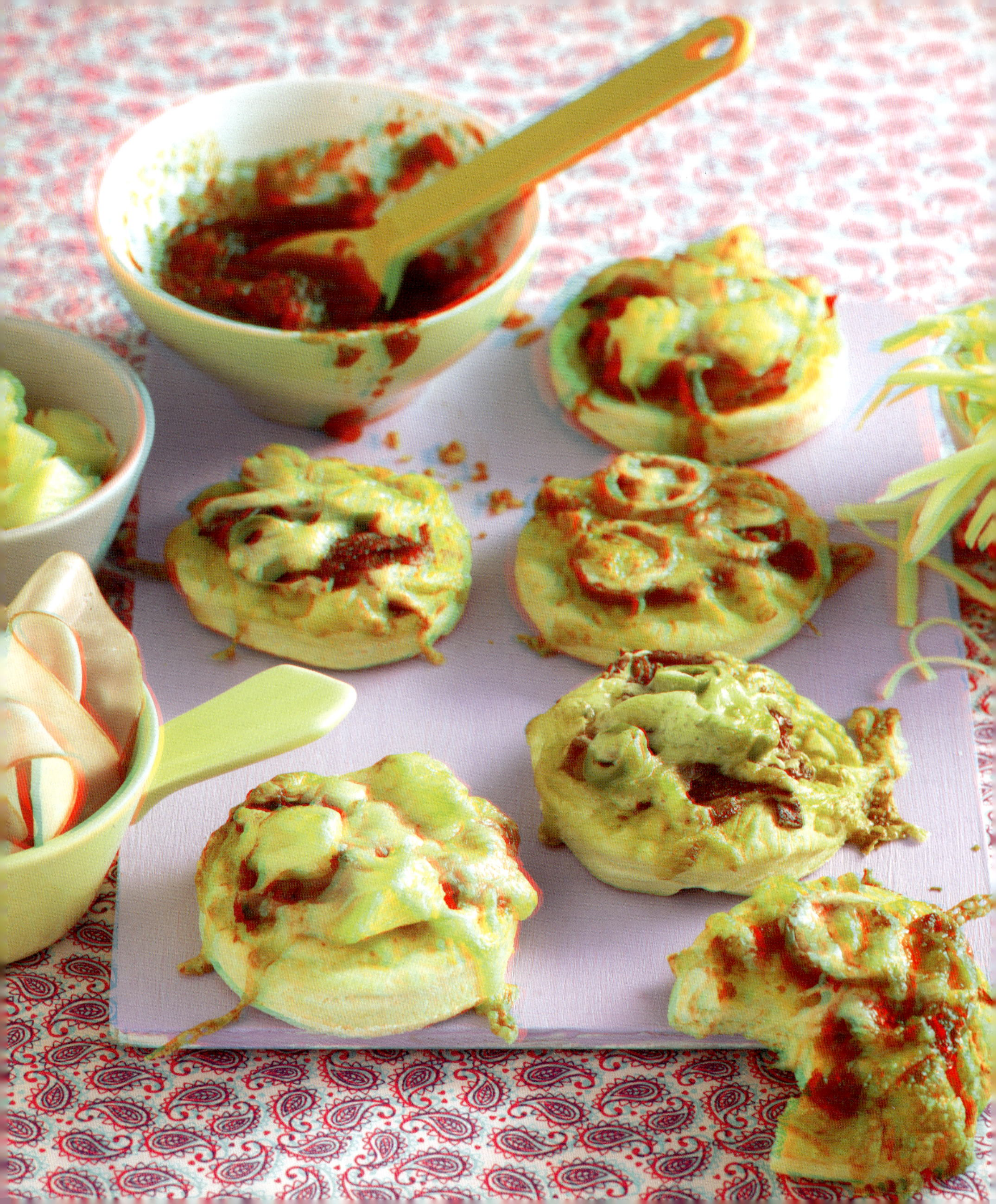

pizzettes

MAKES 12 | **PREP TIME** 30 MINS | **COOKING TIME** 15 MINS

300 g (10½ oz/2 cups) **self-raising flour**
40 g (1½ oz) **butter**, chopped
170 ml (5½ fl oz/⅔ cup) **milk**
60 g (2¼ oz/¼ cup) **pizza sauce**
85 g (3 oz/⅔ cup) grated **tasty cheese**

TOPPING SUGGESTIONS
chopped shaved **ham**
pineapple pieces
sliced **cherry tomatoes**
sliced **salami**
pitted **olives**

1 Preheat the oven to 190°C (375°F/Gas 5). Line a large baking tray with baking paper. Sift the flour into a large bowl and add the butter. Using your fingertips, rub in the butter until well combined.

2 Make a well in the centre and pour in the milk. Use a butter knife to mix together in a cutting motion, until evenly moistened. Gather the dough together with your hands. Turn out onto a lightly floured bench and lightly press together until smooth. Don't knead madly or it will end up being tough. Use a rolling pin to roll out to a 7 mm (¼ inch) thickness.

3 Use an 8 cm (3¼ inch) round cutter to cut rounds from the dough, as close together as possible. Gently press the dough scraps together and lightly re-roll. Cut out more rounds until you get 12 in total.

4 Place the pizza bases onto the prepared tray. Spread each one with a little of the pizza sauce. Arrange your favourite bits and pieces on top and sprinkle with cheese. Bake for 15 minutes, or until cheese is melted and lightly browned. Serve warm.

DINO pasties

MAKES 16 | **PREP TIME** 30 MINS + COOLING | **COOKING TIME** 15–20 MINS

2 teaspoons **olive oil**
1 small **onion**, finely chopped
1 **garlic clove**, crushed
300 g (10½ oz) **minced (ground) lamb**
2 tablespoons **tomato paste (concentrated purée)**
1 **carrot**, grated
155 g (1 cup) **frozen peas**
60 ml (2 fl oz/¼ cup) **vegetable stock**
4 sheets frozen **shortcrust pastry**, thawed
1 **egg**, lightly beaten
2 teaspoons **sesame seeds**

1. Preheat the oven to 200°C (400°F/Gas 6). Line a large baking tray with baking paper.

2. Heat the oil in a non-stick frying pan over medium heat. Cook the onion for 4–5 minutes, or until soft. Add the garlic and cook, stirring, for 1 more minute. Add the lamb and cook for about 5 minutes, breaking up any lumps with a wooden spoon as it cooks.

3. Mix in the tomato paste, carrot, peas and stock, and cook for another 5 minutes. Transfer to a large bowl and leave for 5 minutes, stirring occasionally. Put in the fridge for 10 minutes, or until just cold.

4. Using a 12 cm (4½ inch) cutter (or saucer as a guide), cut four rounds from each sheet of pastry. Place 2 tablespoons of the filling onto a round and bring two sides up to meet on top. Pinch the pastry together, making a frill at the top. Place onto the prepared tray.

5. Brush the pasties with egg and sprinkle with sesame seeds. Bake for 15–20 minutes, or until golden brown. Serve warm.

The filling doesn't have to be chilled, just not warm, as it can make the pastry too soft.

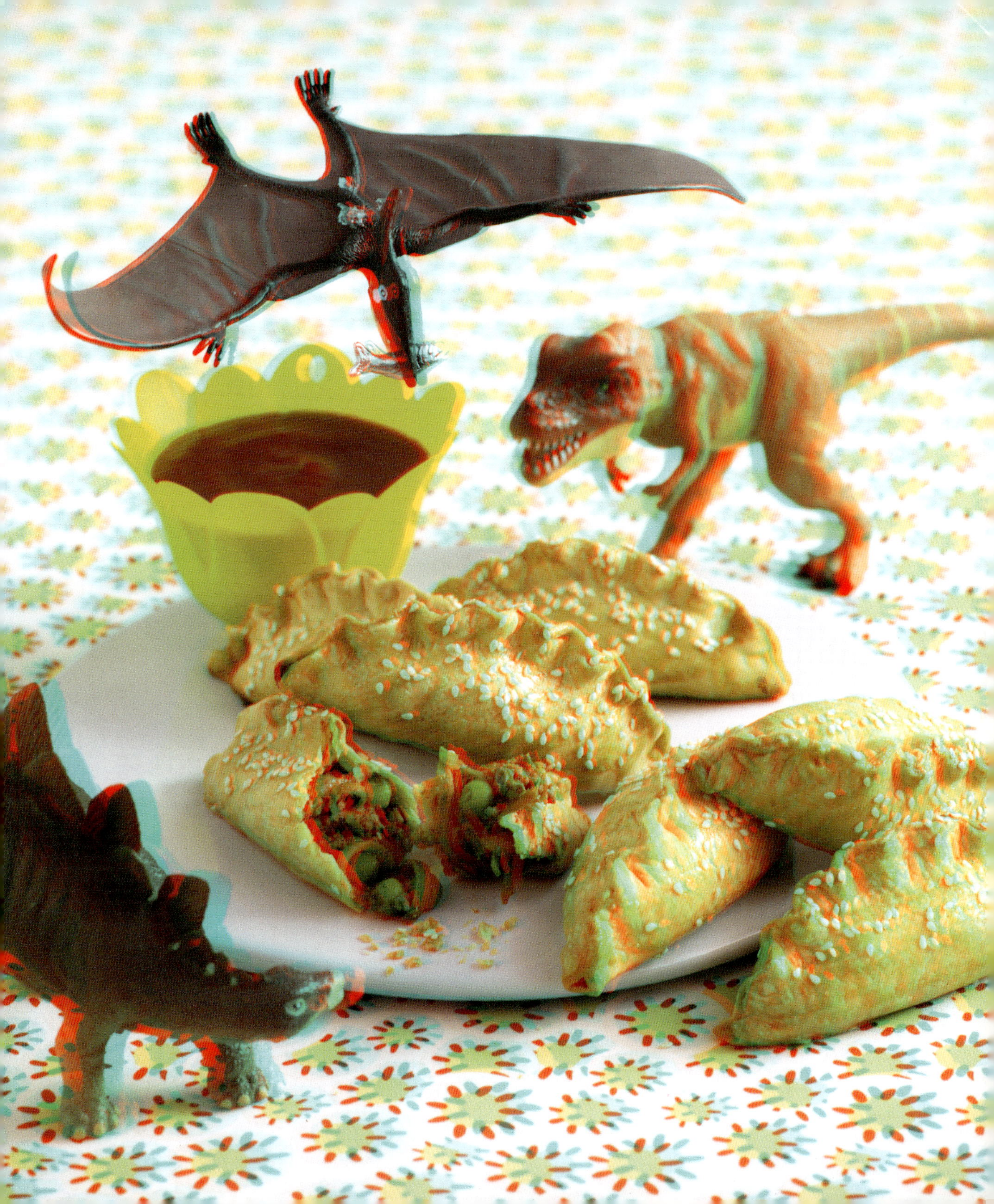

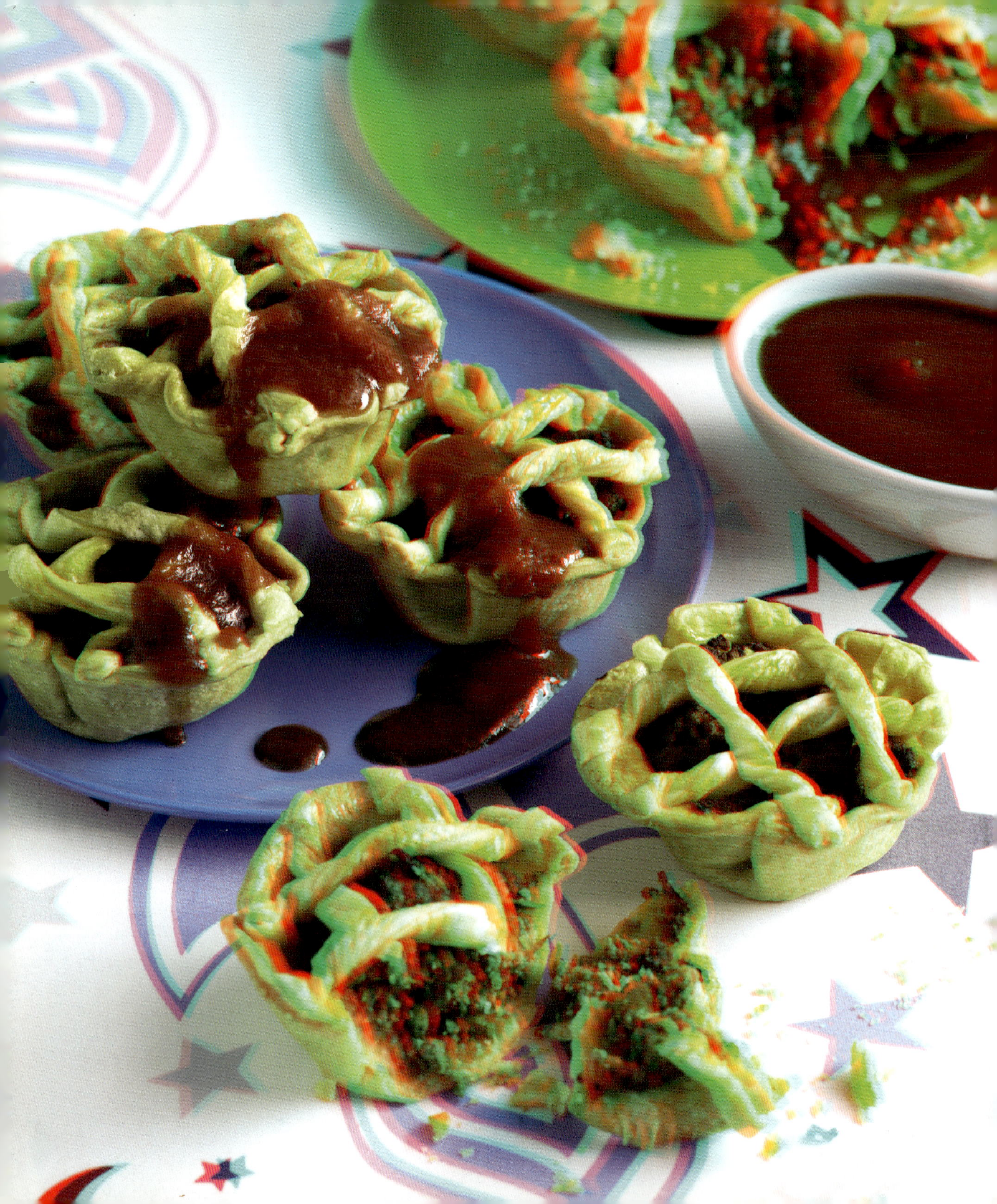

BEEFY pies

MAKES 12 | **PREP TIME** 30 MINS + COOLING | **COOKING TIME** 20–25 MINS

2 teaspoons **olive oil**
500 g (1 lb 2 oz) **minced (ground) beef**
1 **zucchini (courgette)**, grated
160 g (5½ oz/⅔ cup) **tomato pasta sauce**
3 sheets frozen **shortcrust pastry**, thawed
1½ sheets frozen **puff pastry**, thawed
1 **egg**, lightly beaten

1 Heat the oil in a large non-stick frying pan over high heat. Add the beef and cook for 5 minutes, breaking up any lumps with a wooden spoon as it cooks. Add the zucchini and cook, stirring, for 1 minute. Add the pasta sauce and stir to combine. Transfer to a large bowl and leave for 5 minutes, stirring occasionally to release the heat. Put in the fridge for 10 minutes, or until just cold.

2 Preheat the oven to 190°C (375°F/Gas 5). Using an 11 cm (4¼ inch) cutter, cut four rounds from each sheet of shortcrust pastry.

3 Brush 12 x 80 ml (2½ fl oz/⅓ cup capacity) muffin holes with oil. Gently ease the pastry rounds into the holes (it will stick up above the edges, but shrink during cooking). Fill with the cooled beef mixture.

4 Cut the puff pastry into 1 cm (½ inch) strips, then cut each strip in half. Twist a strip of pastry and lay across a pie, pressing onto the shortcrust pastry at the edges. Place one more twisted strip across, then two twisted strips in the opposite direction, to make a criss-cross pattern. Trim the overhanging pastry from the ends. Repeat with remaining pastry and pies.

5 Brush the pastry strips with egg. Bake for 20–25 minutes, or until golden brown. Cool in the tin for 5 minutes, then use a butter knife to lift the pies from the tins. Serve warm.

corn fritters

MAKES ABOUT 12 | **PREP TIME** 10 MINS | **COOKING TIME** 3 MINS PER BATCH

420 g (15 oz) tinned **corn kernels**, drained
75 g (2½ oz/½ cup) **self-raising flour**
2 tablespoons finely grated **parmesan cheese**
2 **spring onions (scallions)**, finely sliced
2 **eggs**, lightly beaten
2 tablespoons **milk**
vegetable oil, to shallow-fry
1 small ripe **avocado**
1 teaspoon **lemon juice**
6 **cherry tomatoes**, halved

1. Place the corn, flour, parmesan and onions into a mixing bowl. Make a well in the centre. Add the eggs and use a fork to gently mix until combined.

2. Pour enough oil into a frying pan so that it is 5 mm (¼ inch) deep. Heat over medium heat. Drop slightly heaped tablespoons of mixture into the pan and flatten slightly with the back of a spoon (they should be about 5cm/2 inches in diameter).

3. Cook for 1½ minutes, or until golden brown underneath, then carefully turn and cook the other side for 1½ minutes. Lift from the pan with a slotted spatula and drain on paper towels.

4. Cut the avocado in half and scoop out the flesh into a bowl. Add the lemon juice and mash with a fork. Spread a little of the avocado onto each fritter. Top with a cherry tomato half.

You will only be able to cook about four fritters at a time, depending on the size of your frying pan.

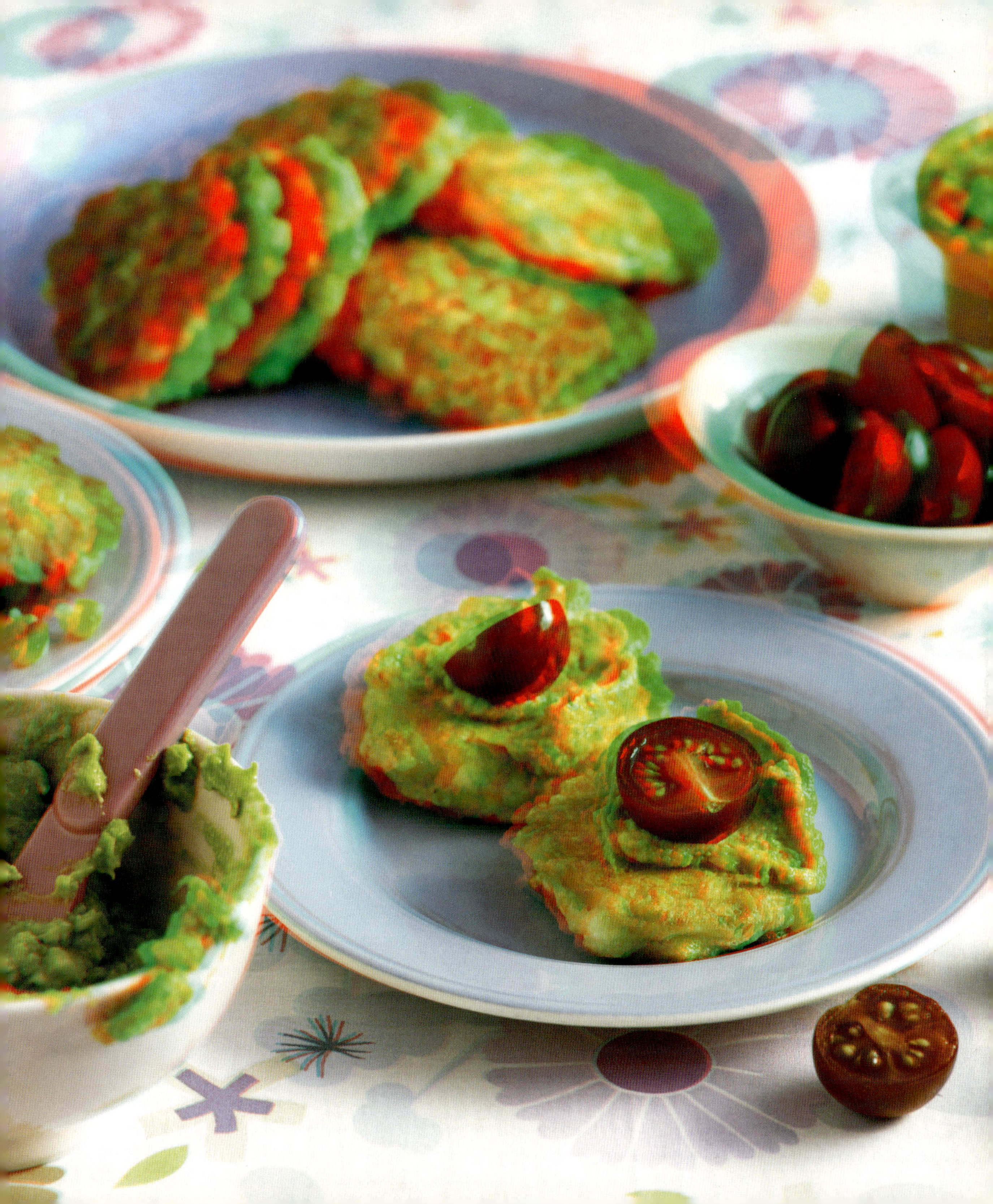

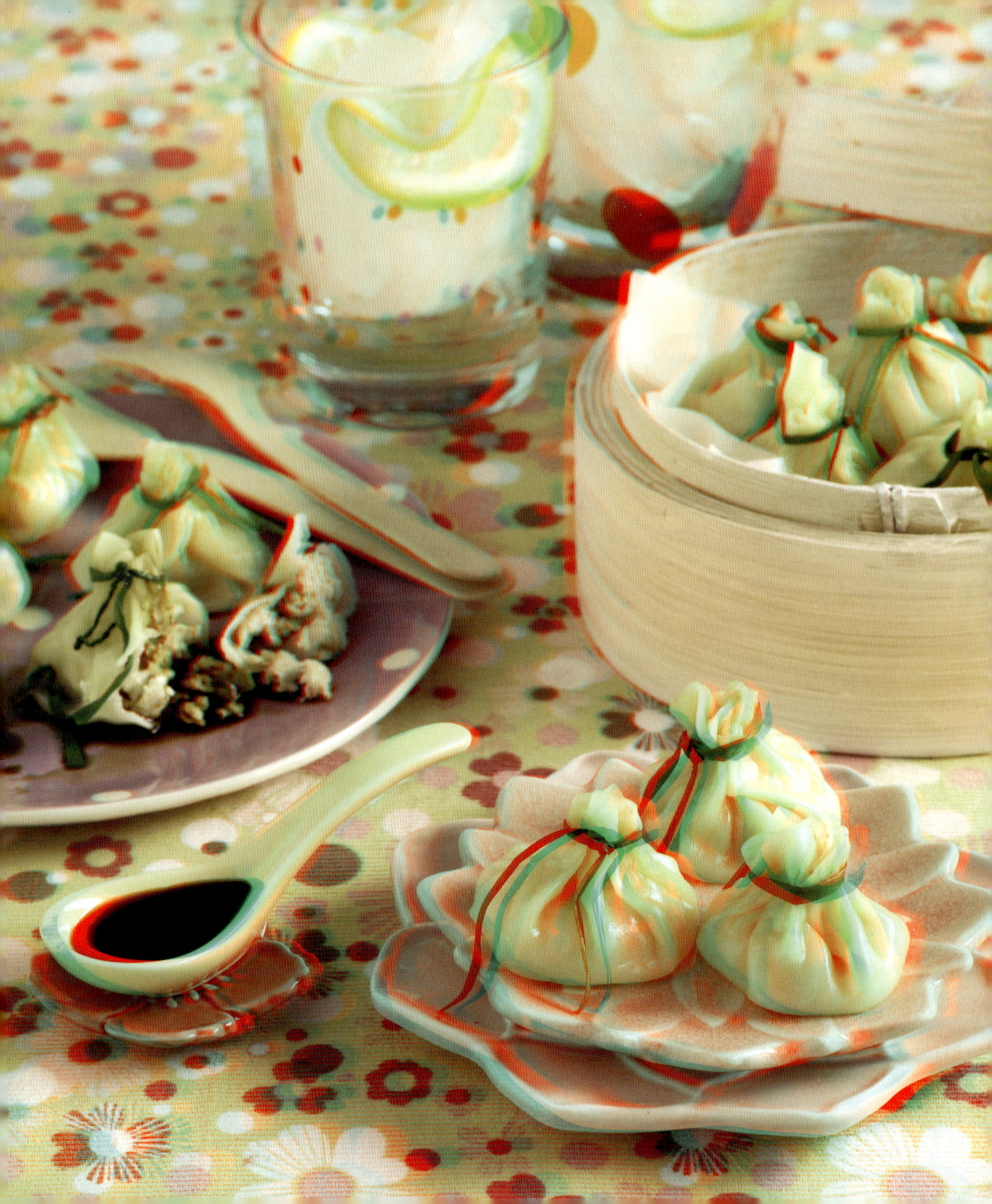

moneybags

MAKES 30 | **PREP TIME** 20 MINS | **COOKING TIME** 10 MINS

300 g (10½ oz) **minced (ground) chicken**
3 **spring onions (scallions)**, finely sliced
1 teaspoon finely grated **ginger**
2 **garlic cloves**, crushed
1 tablespoon **hoisin sauce**
30 round **gow gee wrappers**
1 bunch **chives** (if you like)
soy sauce, for dipping

1. Place the chicken, onion, ginger, garlic and hoisin sauce into a mixing bowl. Use your clean hands to mix well.

2. Lay out a wonton wrapper and place a heaped teaspoon of the mixture into the middle. Gather the sides up and pinch together to make a little pouch shape. Repeat with the remaining wrappers and filling.

3. Line a bamboo steamer with a sheet of baking paper. Poke some holes in the baking paper so the steam can come through. Place some of the dumplings into the steamer, not touching each other (you will have to cook them in a couple of batches).

4. Stand the streamer over a wok or large saucepan of simmering water. Cover and cook for 10 minutes, or until the wrappers are tender. Transfer to a plate and cover with foil to keep warm while you cook the rest. If you like, put chives in a bowl and cover with hot water to soften. Drain, then use to tie a bow around each moneybag. Serve with soy sauce for dipping.

san choy bau

SERVES 4 | **PREP TIME** 20 MINS | **COOKING TIME** 10 MINS

50 g (1¾ oz) **rice vermicelli noodles**
2 teaspoons **peanut oil**
3 **spring onions (scallions)**, finely sliced
100 g (3½ oz) **minced (ground) pork**
1 tablespoon **hoisin sauce**
1 small **carrot**, grated
125 g (4½ oz) tinned **corn kernels**, drained
12 small **iceberg lettuce** leaves
sweet chilli sauce and **limes**, to serve

1 Put the noodles in a heatproof bowl and cover with boiling water. Stand for 5 minutes, then rinse under cold running water and drain well. Squeeze out any excess water. Use scissors to chop the noodles a few times, to make them shorter and easier to mix.

2 Heat the oil in a frying pan over medium heat. Add the onion and cook for 2 minutes, or until soft. Add the pork and cook, stirring, for 5 minutes, breaking up any lumps with a wooden spoon.

3 Stir in the hoisin sauce, carrot and corn. Cook, stirring occasionally, for another 2–3 minutes, or until the carrot is soft. Cool slightly and mix with the noodles. Divide the mixture between the lettuce leaves. Serve straight away, with sweet chilli sauce and limes, for squeezing.

You can replace the pork mince with a small tin of tuna, drained. Don't worry about cooking. Mix all the filling ingredients, except for the oil and hoisin sauce. Add 1 tablespoon each of sweet chilli sauce and lime juice.

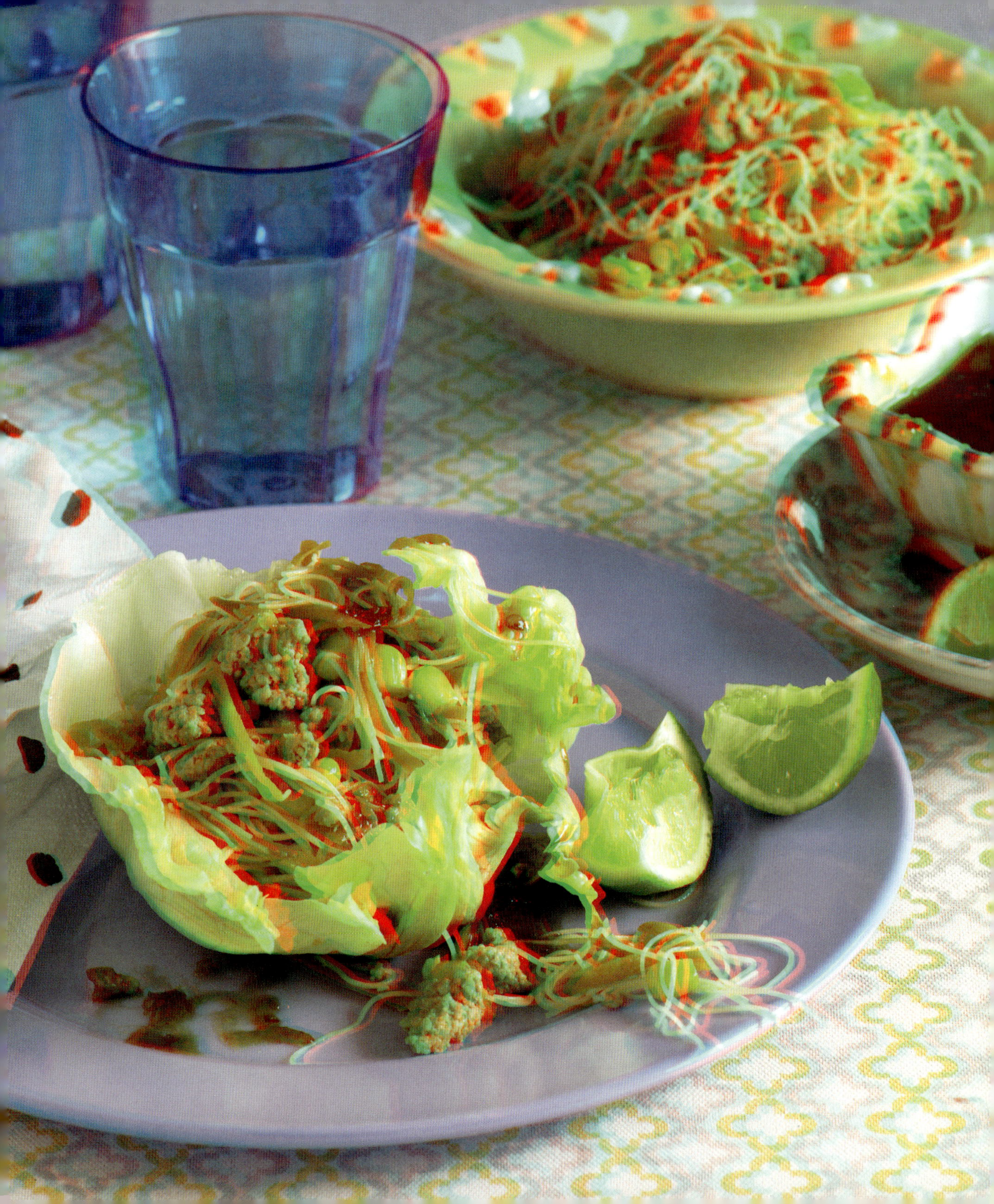

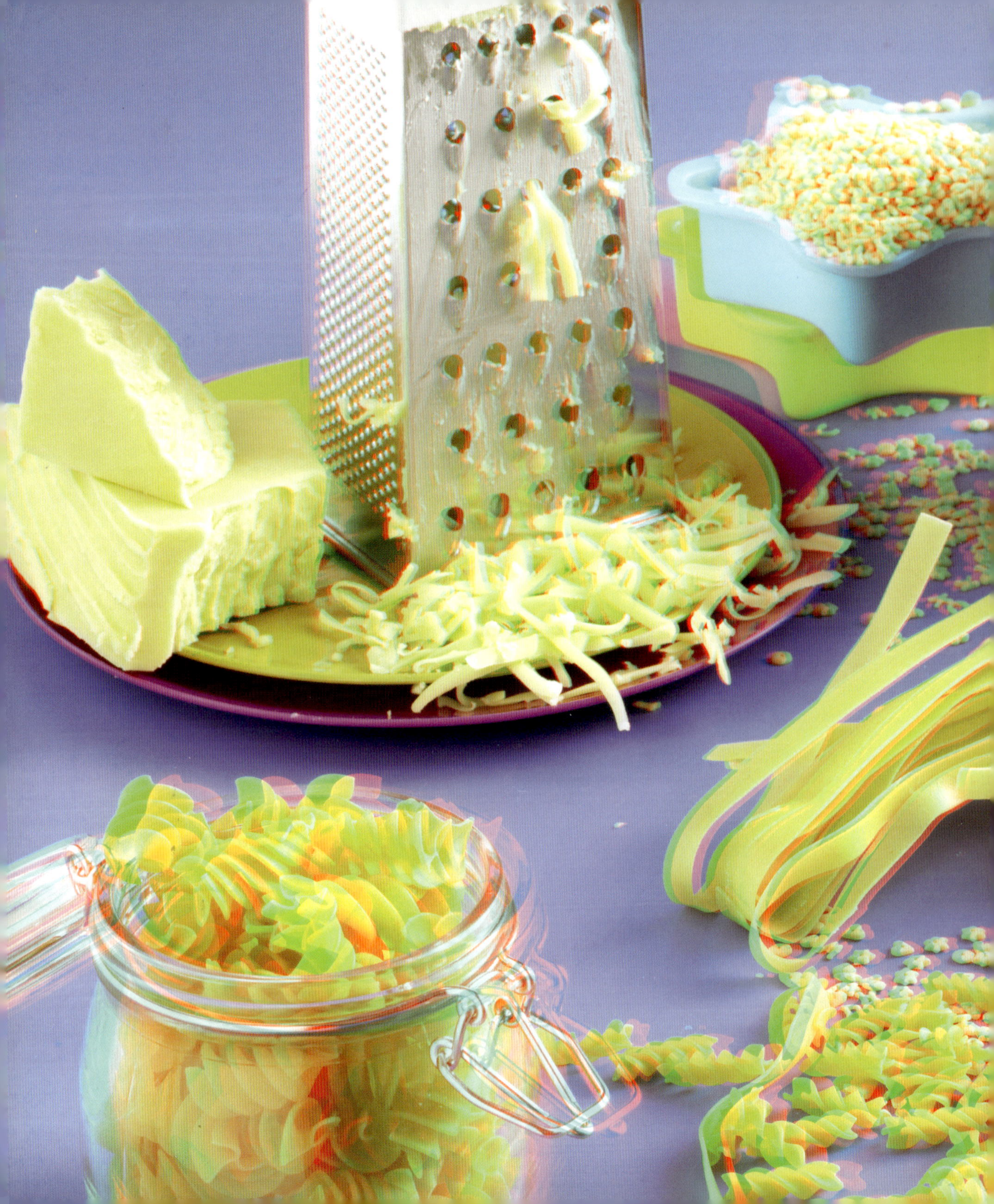

BIG BITES

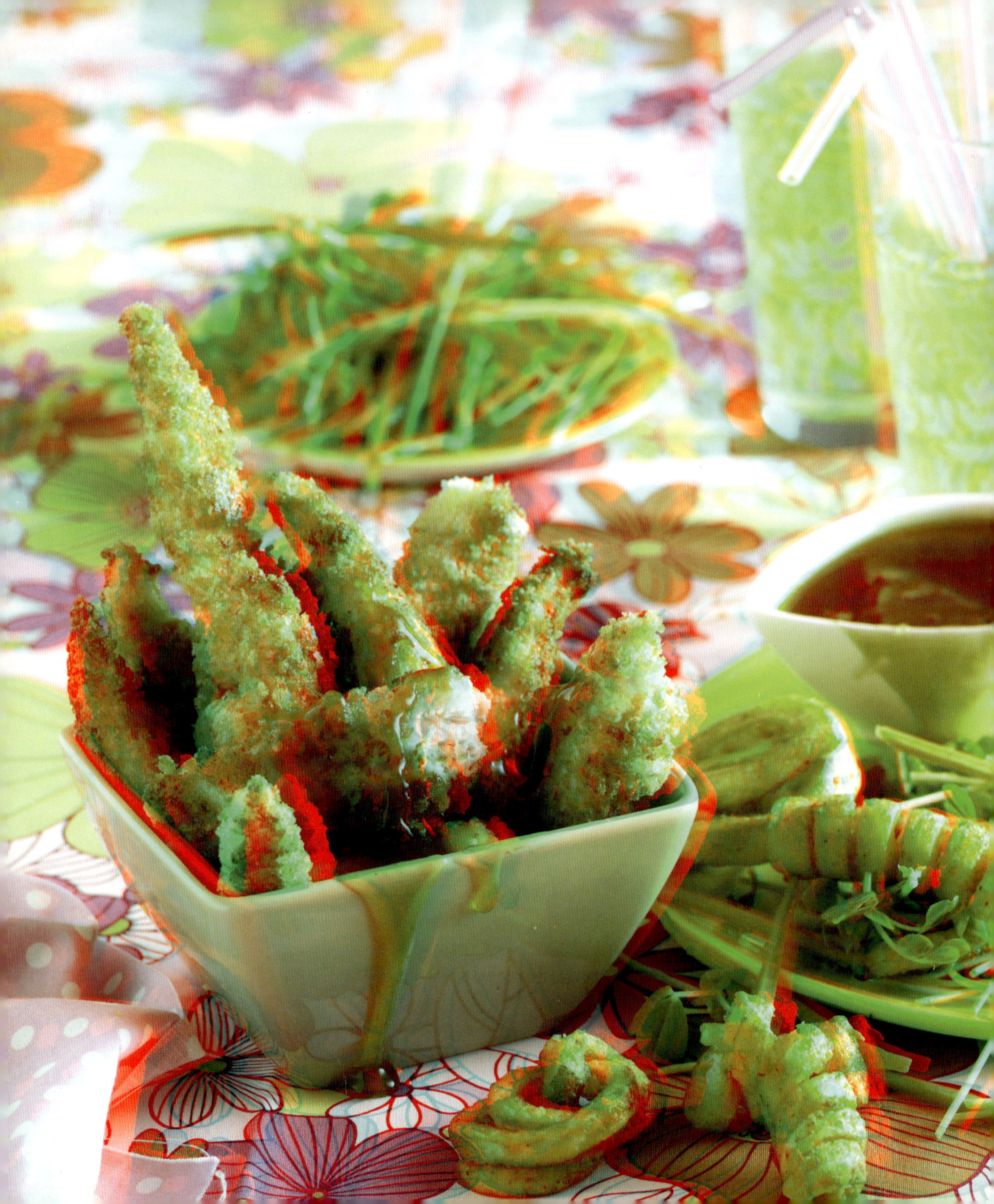

CRUNCHY chicken fingers

SERVES 4 | **PREP TIME** 30 MINS | **COOKING TIME** 20 MINS

2 **eggs**
40 g (1½ oz/⅓ cup) **plain (all-purpose) flour**
240 g (8½ oz/3 cups) **fresh breadcrumbs**
65 g (2¼ oz/⅔ cup) finely grated **parmesan cheese**
6 **chicken tenderloins**
vegetable oil, to shallow-fry
purchased frozen **curly fries**, baked in the oven to packet directions
salad, to serve
sweet and sour sauce, to serve

1 Break the eggs into a shallow bowl and lightly whisk with a fork. Spread the flour onto a plate. Mix half the breadcrumbs and half the parmesan together in a large bowl.

2 Cut the tenderloins in half diagonally. Coat all over with flour, then gently shake off the excess. Working one at a time, dip into the egg to coat all over and let the egg coating drip back into the bowl.

3 Place into the breadcrumb mixture and press gently, turning to coat both sides. Handle gently so the breadcrumbs don't get mushy. Lay onto a plate and repeat with the remaining chicken. Wipe out the bowl and combine the remaining breadcrumbs and parmesan to finish all the chicken (if you put it all in at first it gets too messy to handle).

4 Pour enough oil into a frying pan so that it is 5 mm (¼ inch) deep. Heat over medium heat. Cook the chicken in 2 batches, for 3 minutes each side (add a little bit more oil between batches). Drain on paper towels. Serve with the curly fries, salad and sweet and sour sauce.

To make fresh breadcrumbs, tear crusts from day-old sliced bread (you'll need about 10 'toast' slices) and whizz in a food processor until fluffy crumbs form. You could use dry breadcrumbs if you like.

LAMB AND vegie kebabs

MAKES 8 | **PREP TIME** 20 MINS + 20 MINS SOAKING | **COOKING TIME** 10–15 MINS

1 large **red capsicum (pepper)**
1 **zucchini (courgette)**
350 g (12 oz) diced **lamb leg**
16 **grape** or small **cherry tomatoes**
2 tablespoons **olive oil**
1 tablespoon **lemon juice**
1 **garlic clove**, crushed
steamed rice, to serve

1 Place 12 bamboo skewers into a shallow dish and cover with water. Leave to soak for about 20 minutes. This helps to stop the skewers burning when cooking. Cut the capsicum into large, flat pieces, then cut into 2 cm (3/4 inch) squares. Cut the zucchini in half lengthways, then into 1.5 cm (5/8 inch) slices.

2 Thread the vegetables and meat onto the skewers. Mix the oil, lemon juice and garlic together and brush over the meat and vegies.

3 Heat a large frying pan or barbecue flatplate. Cook the skewers for 10–15 minutes over medium–high heat, or until the meat is cooked through. Serve straight away, with some steamed rice if you like.

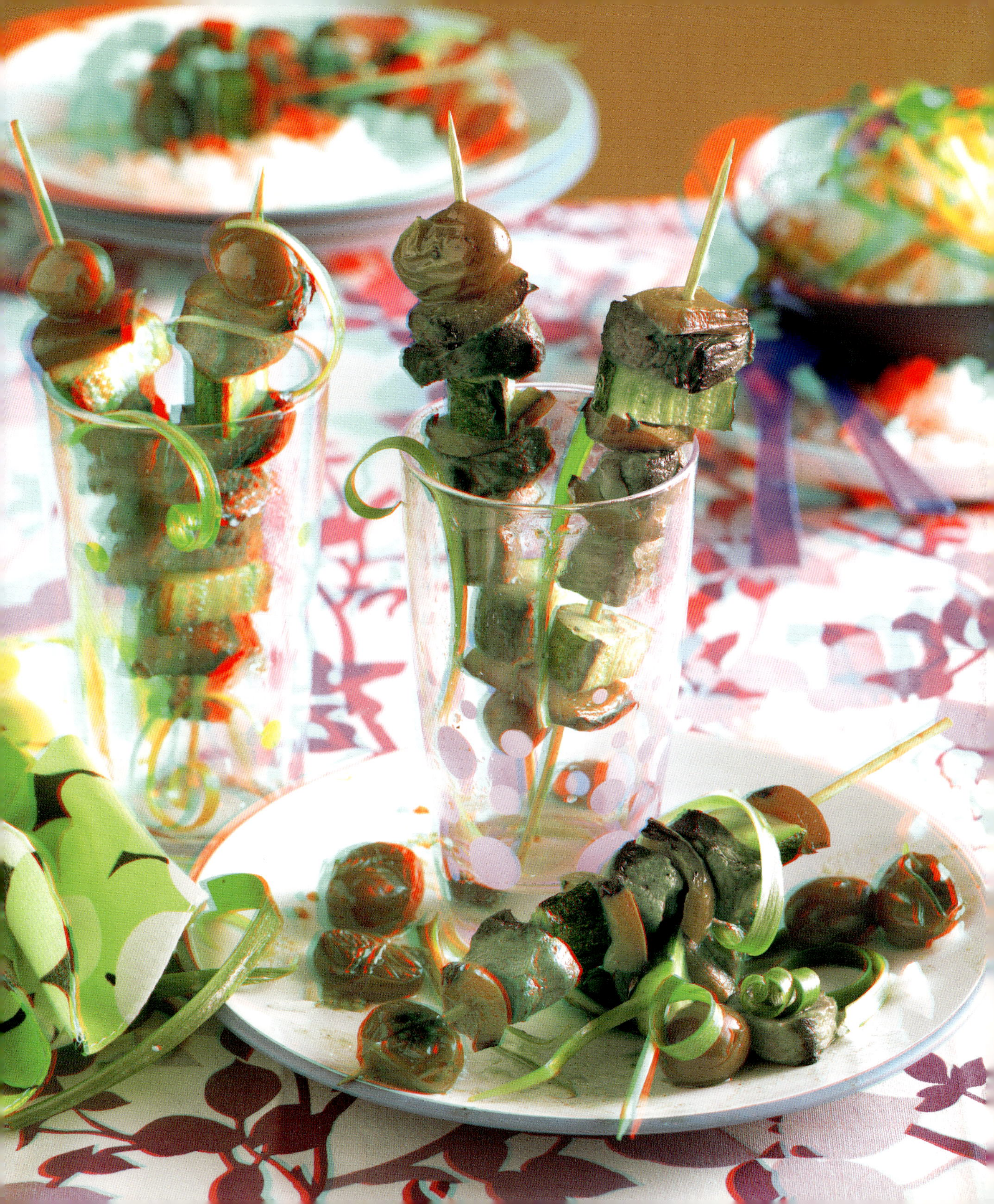

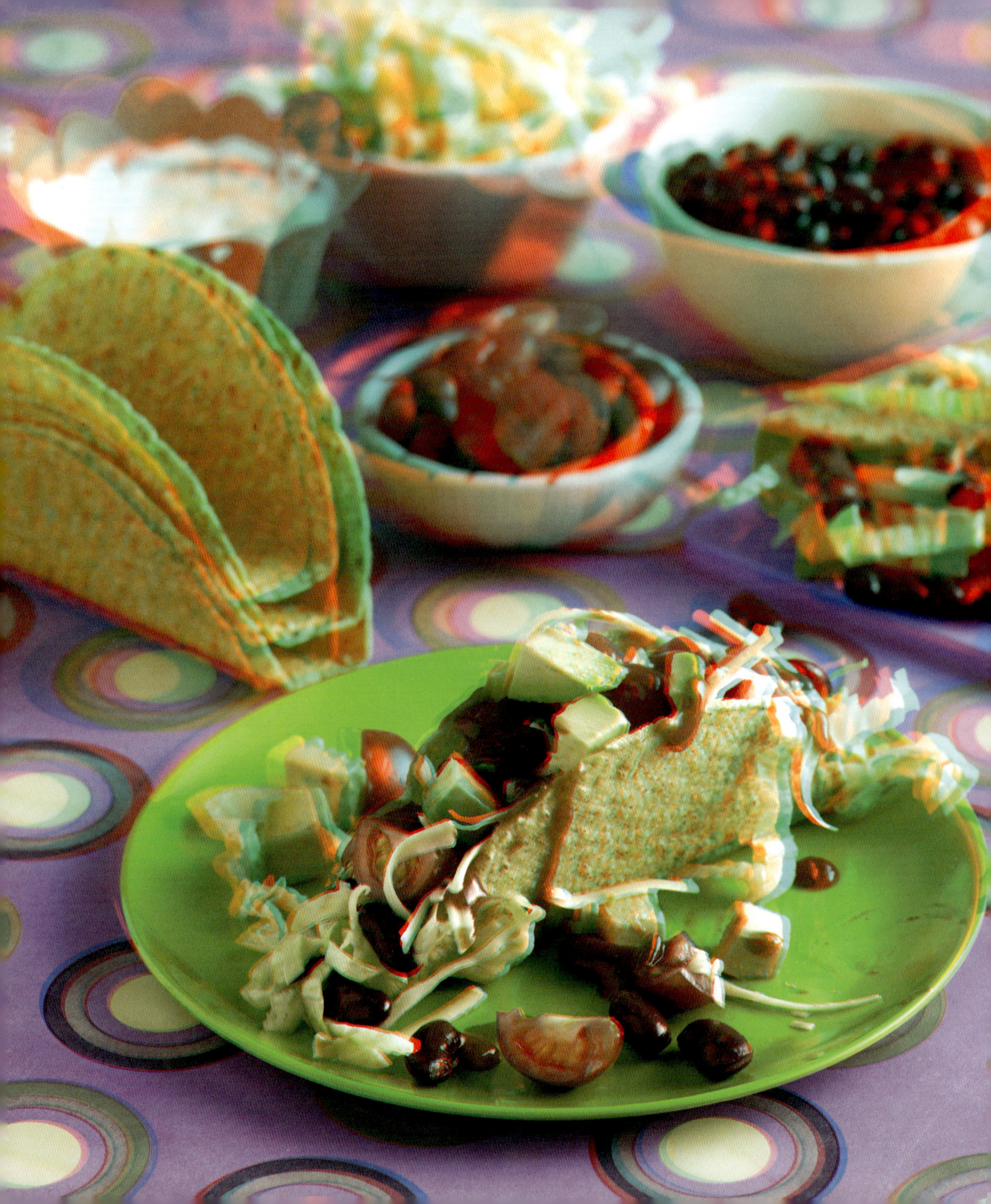

BEAN tacos

MAKES 10 | **PREP TIME** 20 MINS | **COOKING TIME** 7 MINS

10 standing **taco shells**
400 g (14 oz) tinned **kidney beans**, rinsed and drained
125 g (4½ oz/½ cup) **mild taco sauce**
2 large handfuls shredded **iceberg lettuce**
2 **tomatoes**, chopped
1 **avocado**, flesh chopped
250 g (9 oz/2 cups) grated **tasty cheese**

1 Heat the taco shells in the oven, following packet directions. Meanwhile, mix the beans and taco sauce together in a small saucepan and stir over low heat until warm.

2 To assemble, put some lettuce into a taco shell, and top with the bean mixture, tomato, avocado and cheese. Serve straight away.

If you like, you can replace the beans with shredded BBQ chicken or chopped cooked sausages, or add other fillings like sprouts, thin strips of capsicum (pepper) or grated carrot.

CHICKEN coleslaw burgers

SERVES 4 | **PREP TIME** 20 MINS | **COOKING TIME** 12 MINS

2 slices **bread**, crusts removed
500 g (1 lb 2 oz) **minced (ground) chicken**
1 small **onion**, very finely chopped
1 **egg**
1 **garlic clove**, crushed
2 teaspoons **vegetable oil**
4 sesame seed **hamburger buns**
1 small **avocado**
4 **butter lettuce** leaves
1 large **tomato**, sliced
sweet chilli sauce, to serve

COLESLAW
2 handfuls finely shredded **white cabbage**
2 handfuls finely shredded **red cabbage**
1 small **carrot**, grated
2 **spring onions (scallions)**, finely sliced
2 tablespoons **whole-egg mayonnaise**
1 teaspoon **lemon juice**

1 Tear up the bread and place into a food processor. Process until coarse crumbs form. Put the breadcrumbs, chicken, onion and garlic into a bowl and season with salt and pepper. Use your hands to mix together.

2 Divide the mixture into 4 equal portions, and shape into large, flat patties about 10 cm (4 inches) across. Heat the oil in a non-stick frying pan over medium heat. Cook the burgers for 6 minutes on each side.

3 To make the coleslaw, combine the vegies in a bowl. Stir the mayonnaise and lemon juice together, then add to the vegies and toss.

4 Meanwhile, cut the rolls in half, and toast under the grill. Spread the bases with avocado, and top with the lettuce, burger, tomato and coleslaw. Drizzle with sweet chilli sauce, and replace the top.

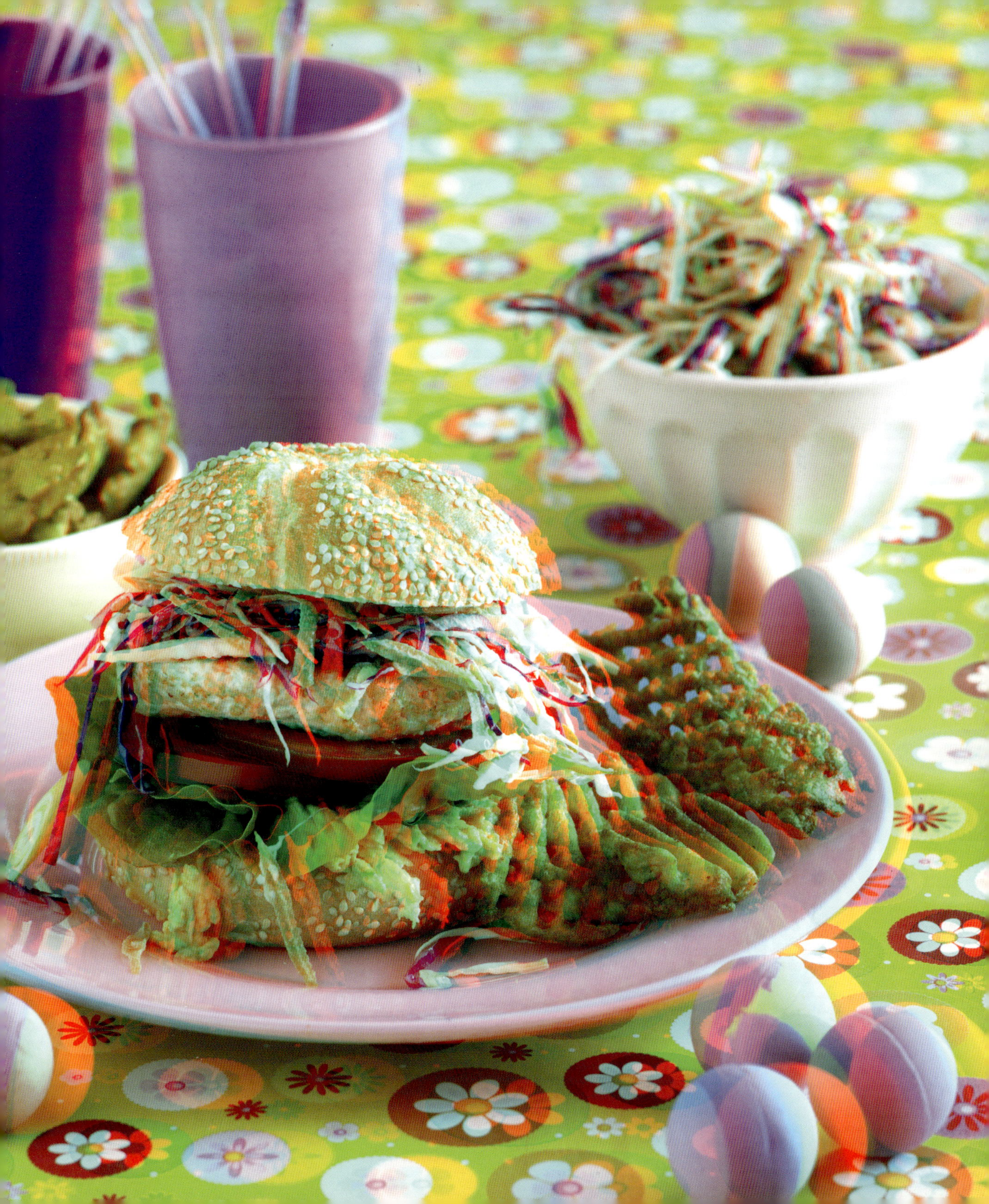

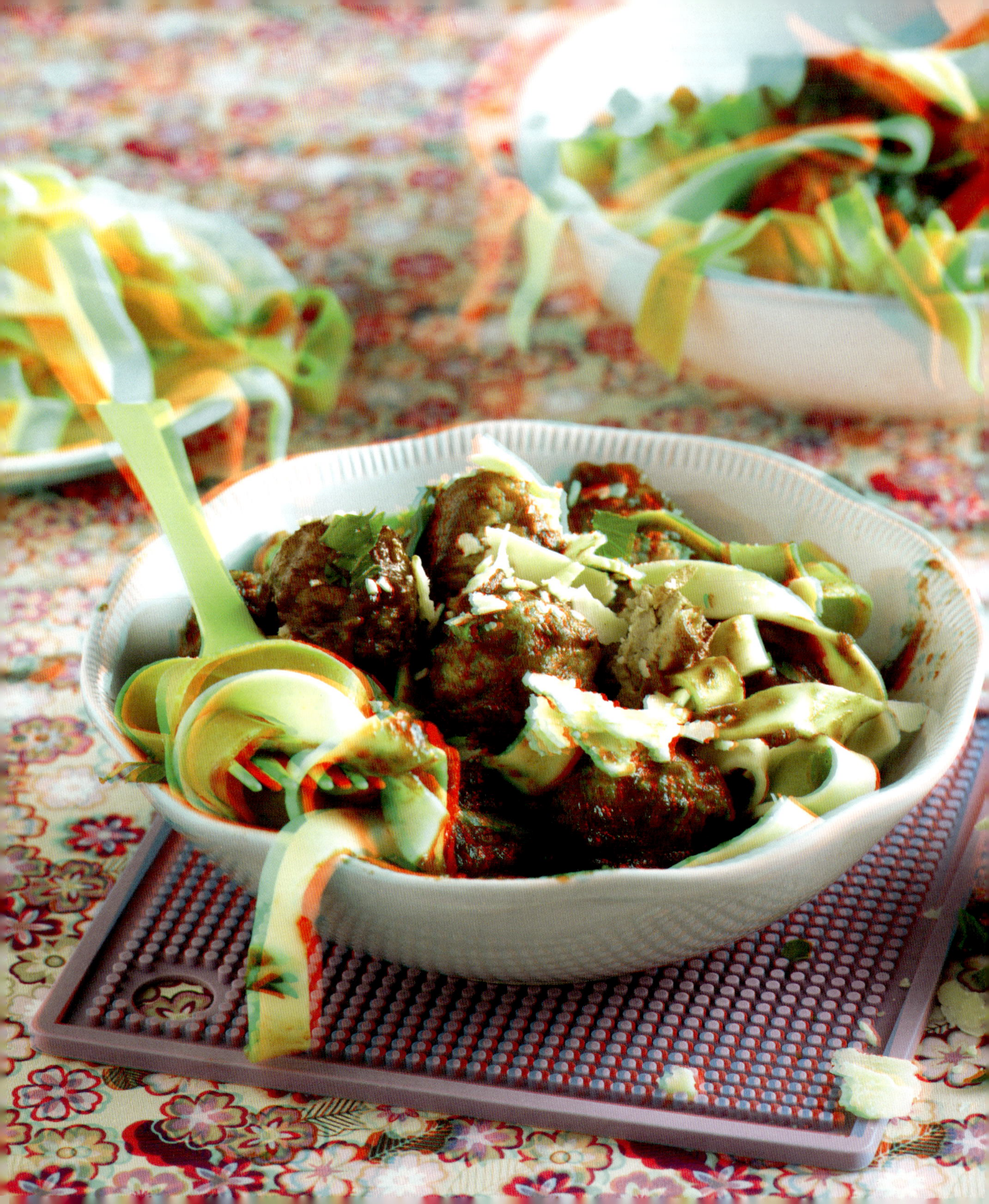

PASTA WITH meatballs

MAKES 4 | PREP TIME 20 MINS | COOKING TIME 12 MINS

350 g (12 oz) **minced (ground) pork**
½ small **onion**, finely chopped
1 small **carrot**, grated
2 tablespoons grated **parmesan cheese**
2 tablespoons **dry breadcrumbs**
1 tablespoon **olive oil**
375 g (13 oz) **fettucine pasta**
375 g (13 oz/1½ cups) **passata (puréed tomatoes)**
shaved **parmesan cheese** and chopped **parsley**, to serve

1 Combine the pork, onion, carrot, parmesan and breadcrumbs in a bowl. Use your hands to mix together. Roll level tablespoons of the mixture into balls.

2 Heat the oil in a large, deep frying pan over medium heat. Cook the meatballs for 10 minutes, turning occasionally, until well browned and cooked through. Add the passata and cook for 2 minutes, or until heated through.

3 Meanwhile, cook the pasta in a large saucepan of salted boiling water following packet directions, until *al dente*. Drain well.

4 Divide the pasta between serving bowls. Top with the meatballs and sauce and sprinkle with parmesan and parsley. Serve straight away.

Passata is an Italian tomato cooking sauce. It's available at the supermarket.

VEGIE AND noodle stir-fry

SERVES 4 | PREP TIME 20 MINS | COOKING TIME ABOUT 5 MINS

450 g (1 lb) packet **hokkien noodles**
1 tablespoon **peanut oil**
2 **carrots**, peeled, halved and thinly sliced diagonally
½ head **broccoli**, cut into small florets
1 **red capsicum (pepper)**, thinly sliced
200 g (7 oz) tinned **baby corn spears**, drained and halved diagonally
2 **garlic cloves**, crushed
4 **spring onions (scallions)**, thinly sliced diagonally
2 tablespoons **kecap manis**
2 tablespoons **lime juice**

1 Place the noodles in a large heatproof bowl and cover with boiling water. Leave for 5 minutes, then use a fork or chopstick to separate the noodles. Drain well.

2 Meanwhile, heat the oil in a wok over medium-high heat. Add the carrot, broccoli, capsicum, corn, garlic and most of the spring onion, and stir-fry for 3 minutes. Add 2 tablespoons water and stir-fry for another 2 minutes, or until the vegies are tender-crisp.

3 Add the noodles, kecap manis and lime juice. Toss to combine and heat through. Divide between serving bowls and serve topped with the remaining spring onion.

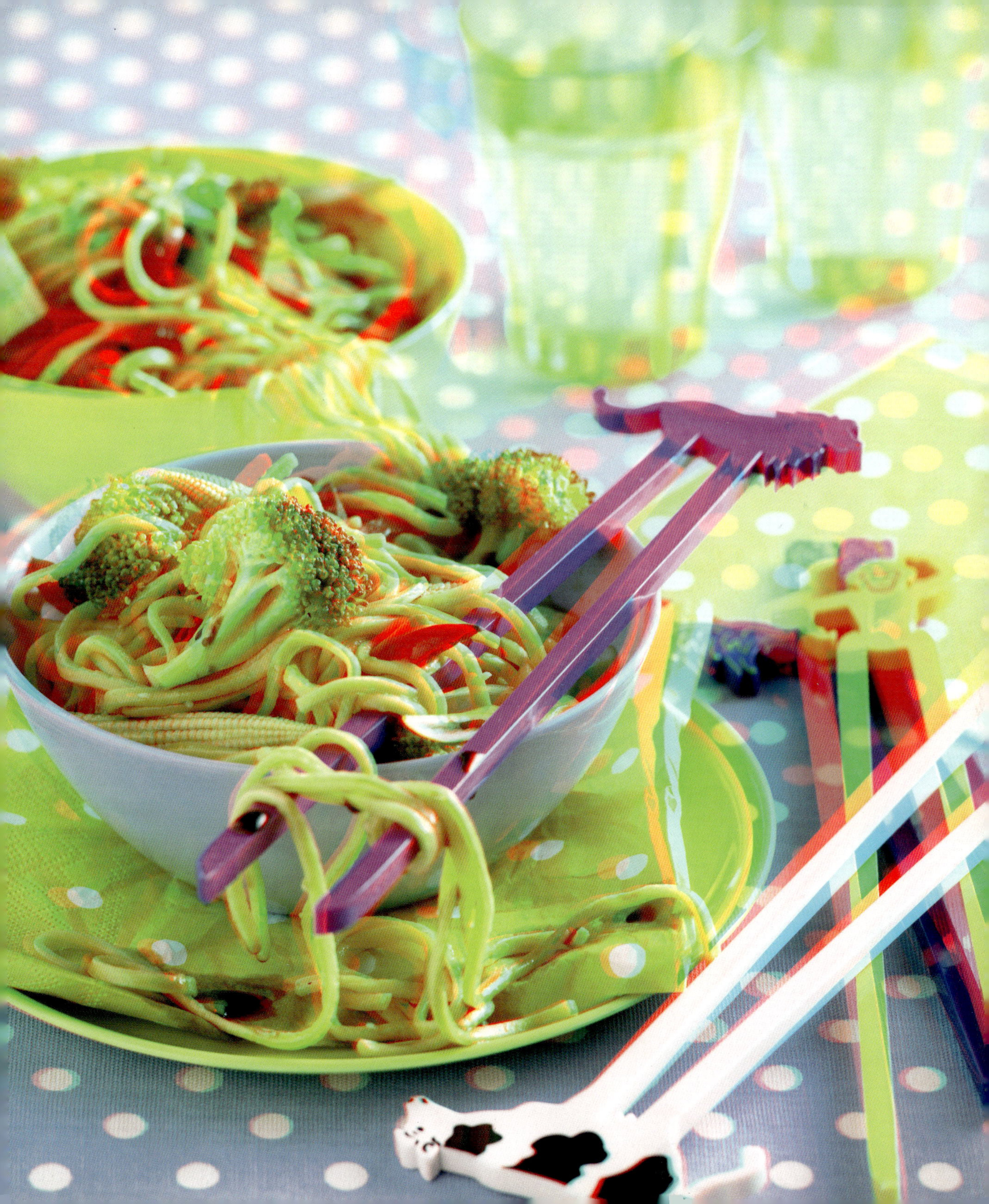

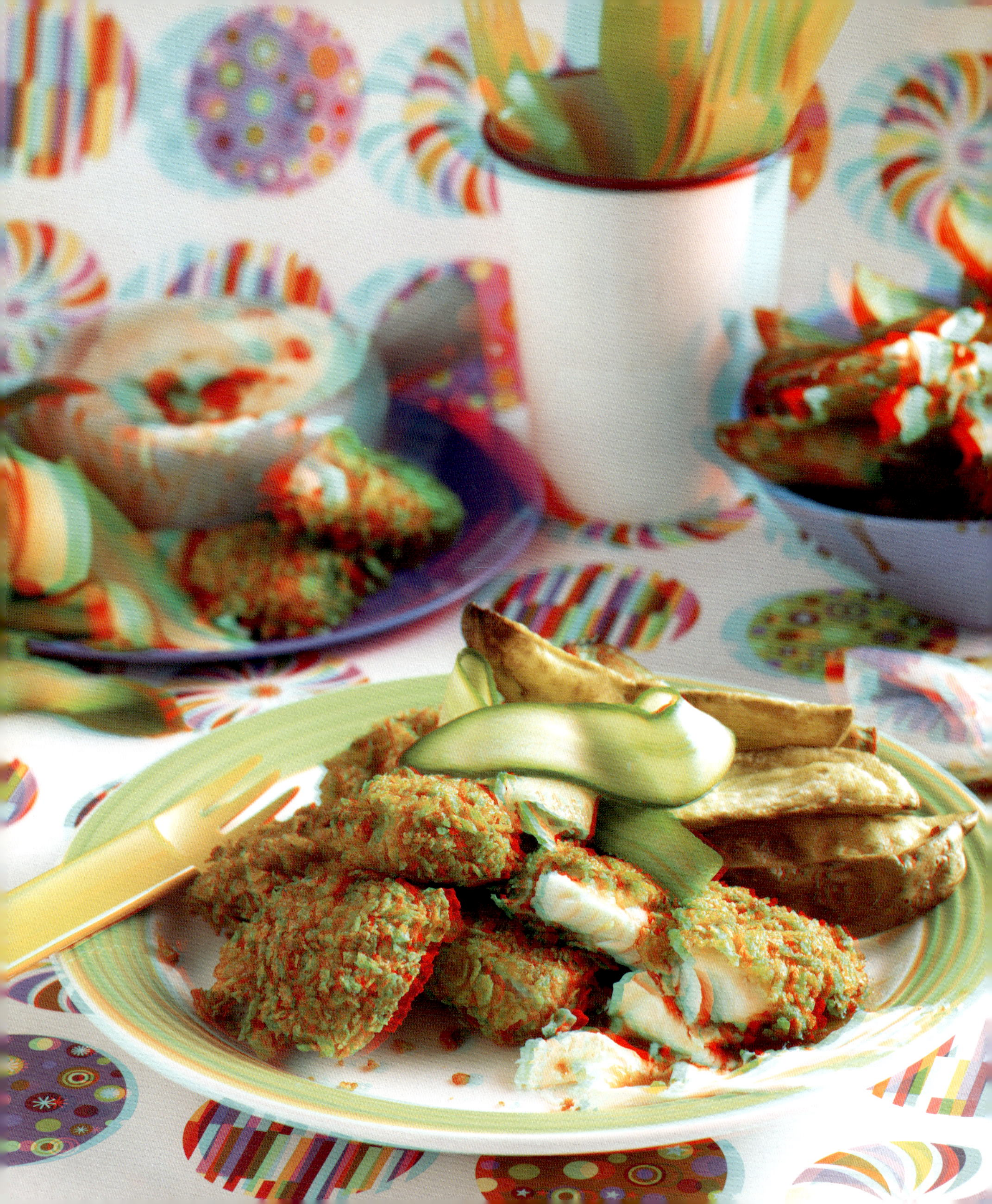

CRISPY FISH NIBBLES
with oven wedges

SERVES 4 | **PREP TIME** 20 MINS | **COOKING TIME** 40 MINS

2 **all-purpose potatoes**, about 200 g (7 oz) each
olive oil spray
400 g (14 oz) boneless **white fish fillets**
4 tablespoons **plain (all-purpose) flour**
2 **eggs**, lightly beaten
120 g (4¼ oz/4 cups) **cornflakes**
1 **cucumber**, peeled into ribbons
sour cream and **sweet chilli sauce**, to serve

1 Preheat the oven to 200°C (400°F/Gas 6) and spray two large non-stick baking trays with oil. Wash the potatoes and cut in half lengthways, then cut each half into 4–6 wedges. Arrange onto one of the trays and spray with oil. Bake for 40 minutes, or until golden brown.

2 Meanwhile, cut the fish into 4 cm (1½ inch) chunks. Place the flour and egg into separate shallow bowls. Place the cornflakes into a large bowl and crush with your hands into small crumbs.

3 Dip all the fish into the flour and shake off the excess. Working with one piece at a time, dip into the egg to coat, then into the cornflake crumbs. Turn and press the fish into the crumbs until evenly coated. Shake off the excess.

4 Place the fish onto the other baking tray and spray with olive oil. Cook for 10–15 minutes, (add it to the oven after the potatoes have been cooking for 30 minutes), or until crisp and cooked through. Serve the fish with the wedges, cucumber ribbons, sour cream and sweet chilli sauce.

CHUNKY SOUP
with cheesy soldiers

SERVES 6 | **PREP TIME** 20 MINS | **COOKING TIME** ABOUT 30 MINS

1 tablespoon **olive oil**
1 **onion**, chopped
3 **celery stalks**, halved lengthways and sliced
2 **carrots**, chopped
400 g (14 oz) tinned diced **tomatoes**
1.5 litre (52 fl oz/6 cups) **vegetable stock**
90 g (3¼ oz/1 cup) **pasta spirals**
1 **chicken breast fillet** (about 250 g/9 oz), cut into 2 cm (¾ inch) cubes
½ loaf **Turkish bread**
125 g (4½ oz/1 cup) grated **tasty cheese**

1 Heat the oil in a large saucepan over medium heat. Add the onion, celery and carrot. Cook for 10 minutes, stirring occasionally, or until soft and lightly golden.

2 Add the tomatoes and stock, cover and bring to the boil. Reduce the heat to medium-low and simmer, with the lid tilted slightly, for 10 minutes.

3 Add the pasta and increase the heat to medium. Return to the boil then cook, again partially covered, for 8 minutes. Add the chicken, return to the boil and cook for another 2 minutes.

4 Meanwhile, cut the bread in half horizontally, then cut each piece into six 'soldiers'. Place onto a baking tray and cook under the grill (broiler) until golden on both sides. Sprinkle with cheese and grill until melted. Serve with the soup.

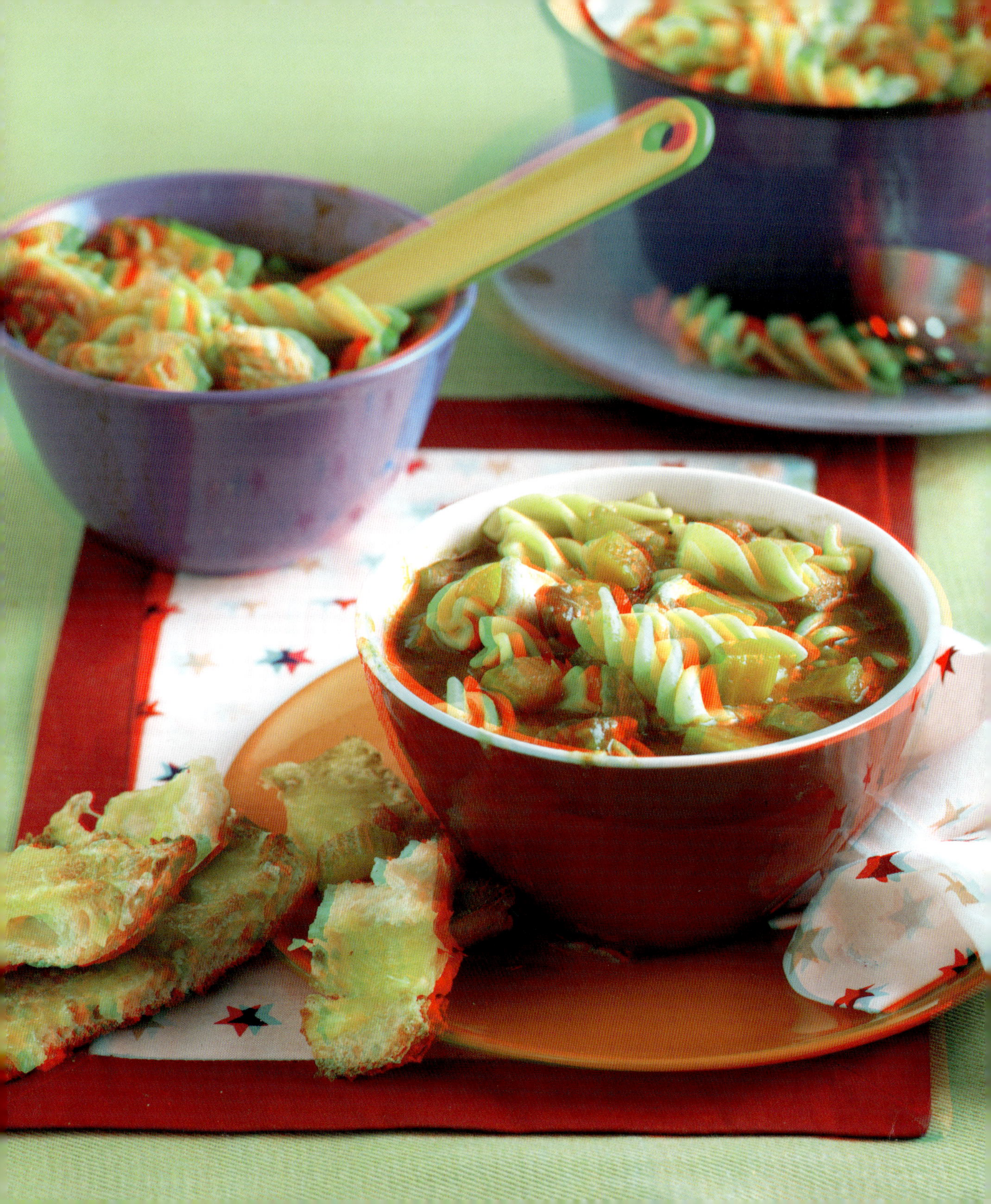

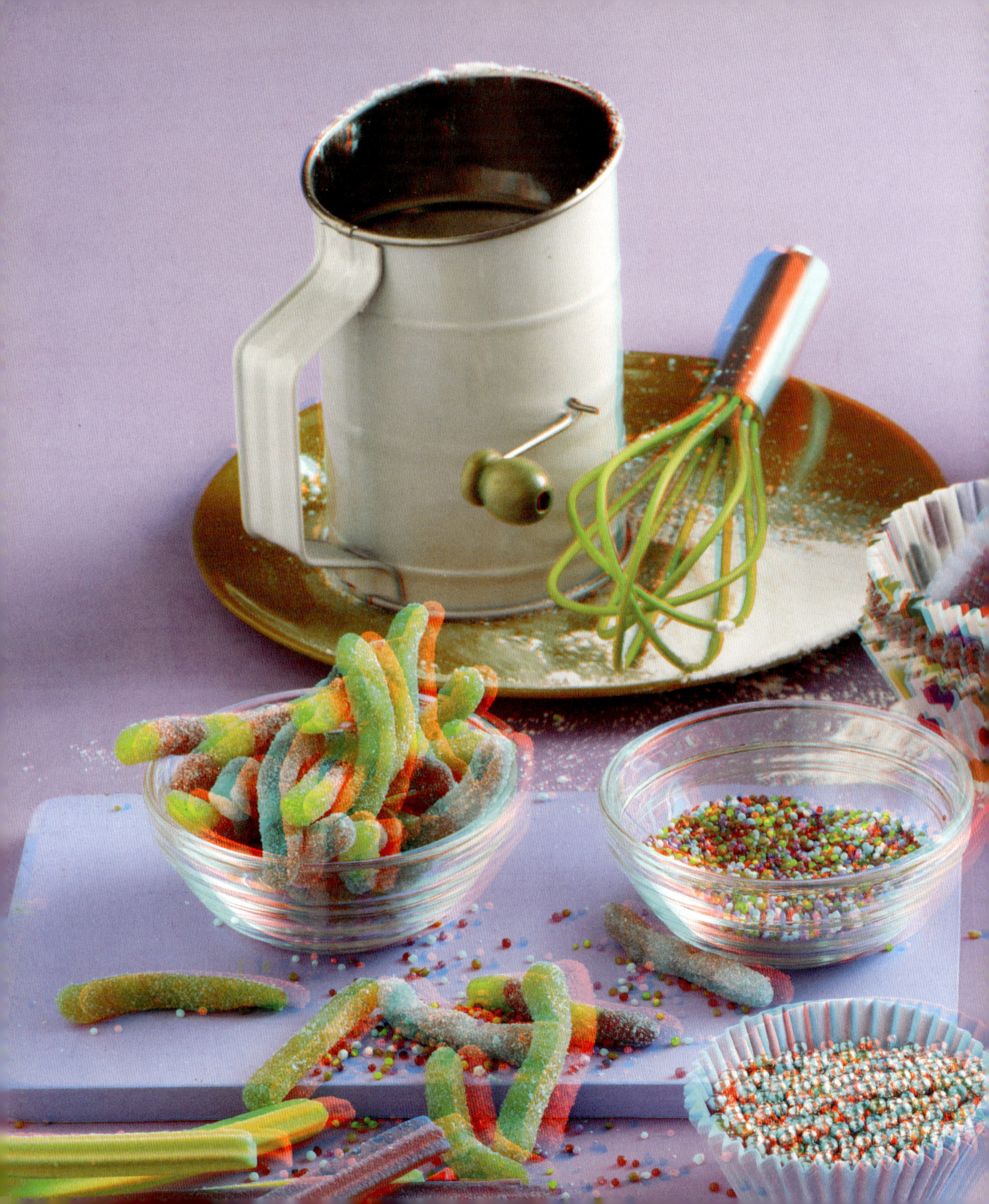

SWEETS

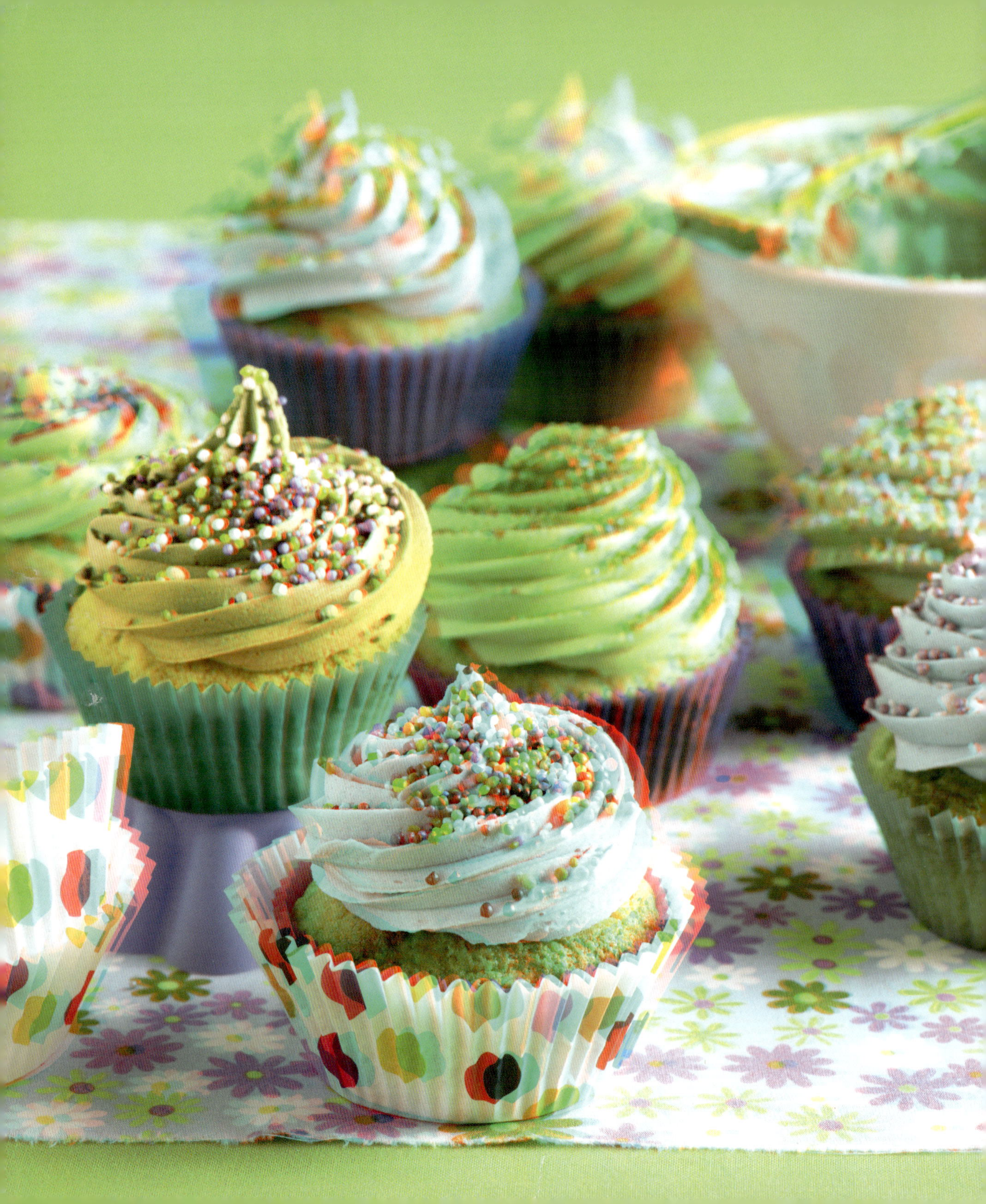

cupcakes

MAKES 12 | **PREP TIME** 40 MINS | **COOKING TIME** 20 MINS

125 g (4½ oz) **butter**, chopped
115 g (4 oz/½ cup) **caster (superfine) sugar**
1 teaspoon **natural vanilla extract**
2 **eggs**
225 g (8 oz/1½ cups) **self-raising flour**
125 ml (4 fl oz/½ cup) **milk**

FROSTING
125 g (4½ oz) **butter**, at room temperature
1 teaspoon **natural vanilla extract**
185 g (6½ oz/1½ cups) **icing (confectioners') sugar**
1 tablespoon **milk**
food colouring of your choice
sprinkles, to decorate

1. Preheat the oven to 180°C (350°F/Gas 4). Line 12 x 80 ml (2½ fl oz/⅓ cup capacity) muffin holes with paper cases. Using electric beaters, beat the butter, sugar and vanilla until light and creamy. Add the eggs one at a time, and beat well after each addition.

2. Fold in the flour and milk until just combined. Spoon into the prepared cases. Bake for 20 minutes, or until they spring back lightly. Transfer to a wire rack to cool completely.

3. To make the frosting, put the butter and vanilla in a mixing bowl. Beat until almost smooth, then add the icing sugar, a little at a time, beating until light and creamy. Beat in the milk.

4. Tint the frosting to your favourite colour. Put the frosting into a piping bag fitted with a 1.5 cm (⅝ inch) fluted nozzle and pipe onto the cakes. Top with sprinkles.

To make different coloured frosting, divide the mixture between several bowls and stir in your colours. You will need to use separate piping bags.

MERINGUE nests

MAKES 8 | **PREP TIME** 20 MINS | **COOKING TIME** 40 MINS + COOLING

3 **egg whites**
170 g (6 oz/¾ cup) **caster (superfine) sugar**
300ml (10½ fl oz) **whipping cream**
1 teaspoon **natural vanilla extract**
fruit, to serve, such as sliced strawberries, kiwifruit, blueberries, raspberries and banana (on their own or in any combination)

1. Preheat the oven to 150°C (300°F/Gas 2). Lightly oil two large baking trays and line with baking paper. Place the egg whites in a large mixing bowl. Using electric beaters, beat until soft peaks form. Add the sugar, about 1 tablespoon at a time, beating until dissolved before you add more. Keep beating until the sugar is all added and the meringue is firm and glossy.

2. Transfer the mixture to a piping bag fitted with a 2.5 cm (1 inch) fluted nozzle. Pipe the mixture to make eight 6 cm (2½ inch) rounds on the trays, leaving plenty of space in between. Smooth the rounds with the back of a spoon to make a firm base. Pipe around the edge of the base to make sides, leaving a space in the middle.

3. Bake for 40 minutes, swapping the trays from top to bottom shelf halfway through cooking. Turn off the oven and prop the door open slightly. Leave in the oven for about 30 minutes, then take out and leave on the tray to cool completely.

4. Using electric beaters, beat the cream and vanilla until soft peaks form. Spoon the cream into the meringues and top with fruit.

You can make the meringues a day ahead. Store in an airtight container in a cool place (not the fridge). Fill with the cream and fruit up to 1 hour before serving.

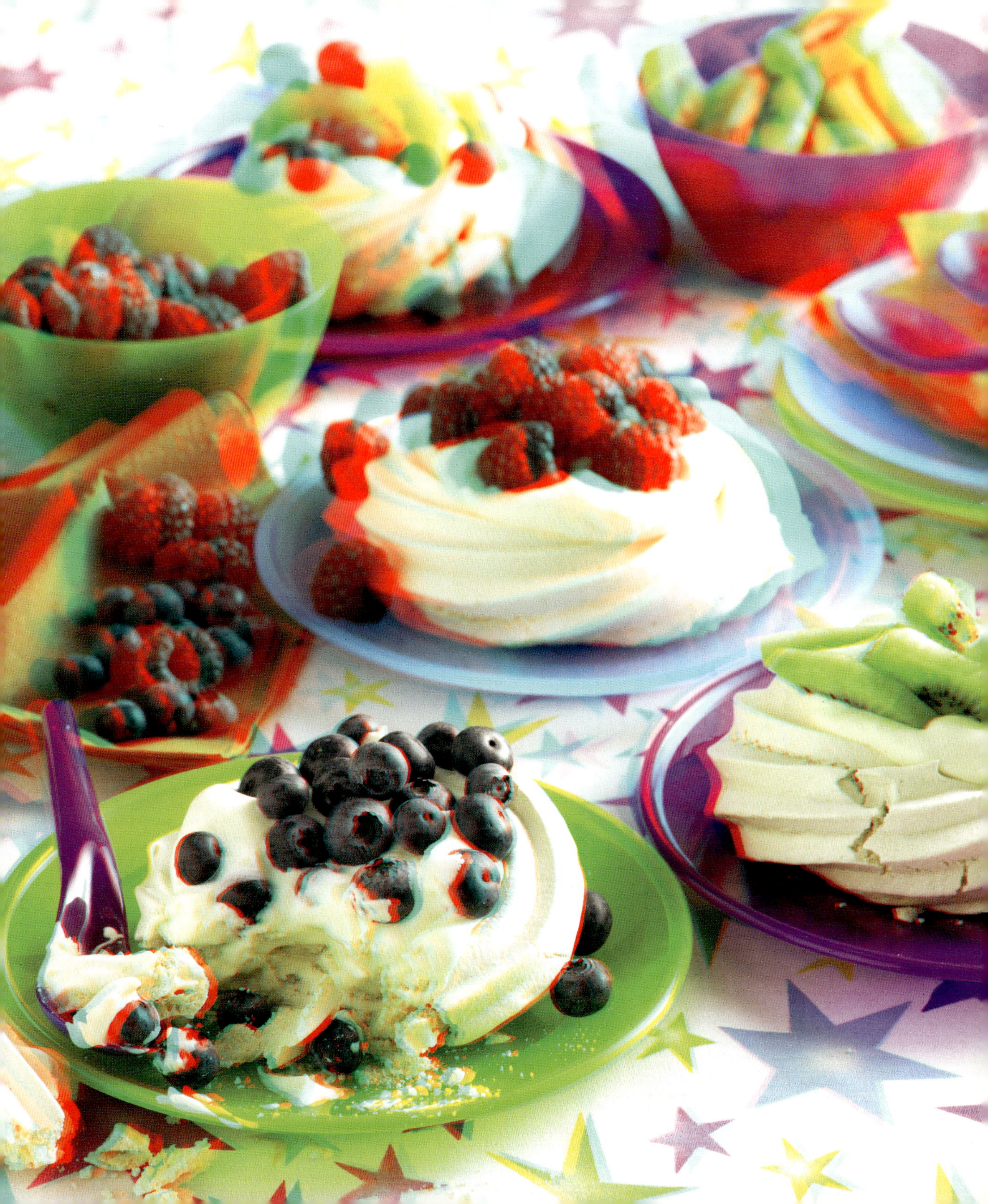

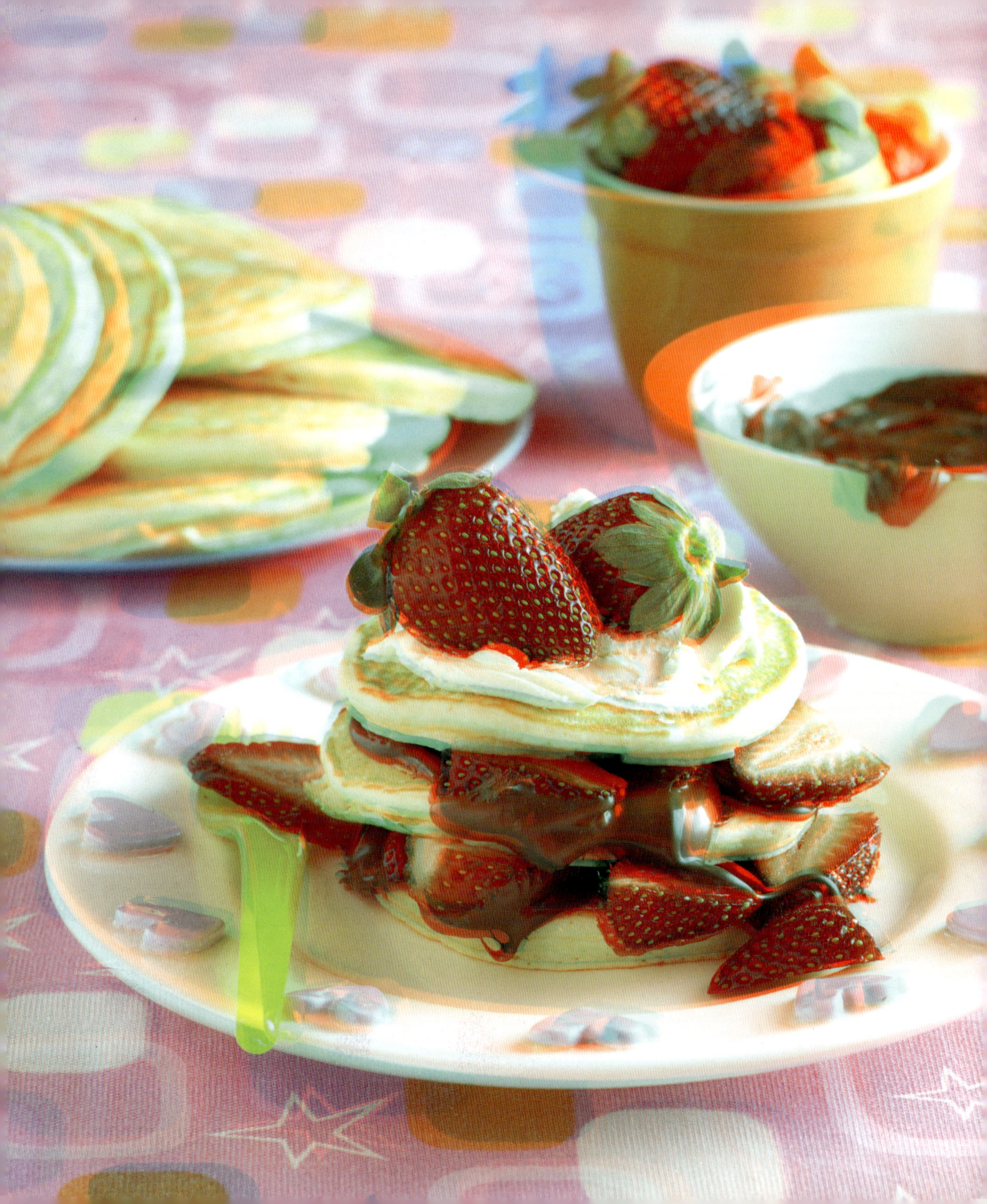

PIKELET stacks

MAKES 15 | **PREP TIME** 10 MINS | **COOKING TIME** 3 MINS PER BATCH

300 g (10½ oz/2 cups) **self-raising flour**
1 teaspoon **baking powder**
2 tablespoons **caster (superfine) sugar**
375 ml (13 fl oz/1 ½ cups) **milk**
2 **eggs**
1 teaspoon **natural vanilla extract**
20 g (¾ oz) cold **butter**
250 g (9 oz) **strawberries**, halved
nutella and **cream cheese**, to serve

1 Sift the flour, baking powder and sugar into a mixing bowl and make a well in the centre. Whisk the milk, egg and vanilla together in a bowl. Pour into the dry ingredients and stir gently until just combined.

2 Heat a large non-stick frying pan over medium–low heat. Wrap the cold butter in a piece of paper towel and carefully wipe over the surface of the pan to grease it (the butter will melt slightly through the paper towel).

3 Drop 2 tablespoonfuls of mixture into the pan and spread out to 9 cm (3½ inches) across. Repeat to make two more in the pan (not too close together). Cook for 2 minutes, or until bubbles appear on the surface. Turn and cook for another minute, or until golden brown. Transfer to a wire rack while you cook the rest of the pikelets.

4 To serve, place one pikelet on a plate and spread with nutella. Top with some sliced strawberries, then add another pikelet on top. Repeat with another layer. Spread some cream cheese on the top pikelet and add strawberries to decorate.

CHUNKY spotty cookies

MAKES ABOUT 20 | **PREP TIME** 20 MINS | **COOKING TIME** 12–15 MINS

125 g (4½ oz) **butter**, at room temperature
165 g (5¾ oz/¾ cup) soft **brown sugar**
1 teaspoon **natural vanilla extract**
1 **egg**
115 g (4 oz/¾ cup) **plain (all-purpose) flour**
75 g (2½ oz/½ cup) **self-raising flour**
130 g (4¾ oz/¾ cup) **white choc bits**
150 g (5½ oz/¾ cup) **m&m's**

1 Preheat the oven to 170°C (325°F/Gas 3). Line two large baking trays with baking paper.

2 Using electric beaters, beat the butter, sugar and vanilla until light and creamy. Add the egg and beat well. Sift the flours over and mix in first with a non-serrated knife, then with lightly your hands until the mixture just clumps together. Add the white choc bits and 100 g (3½ oz/½ cup) of the m&m's, and mix through with your hands.

3 Take heaped tablespoons of the mixture and roll into balls. Place onto the trays and flatten slightly. Dot the remaining m&m's on top of the cookies. Bake for 12–15 minutes, or until golden around the edges. Leave on the trays for 5 minutes, then transfer to a wire rack to cool.

If not using a fan-forced oven, swap the trays between the upper and lower shelves halfway through cooking.

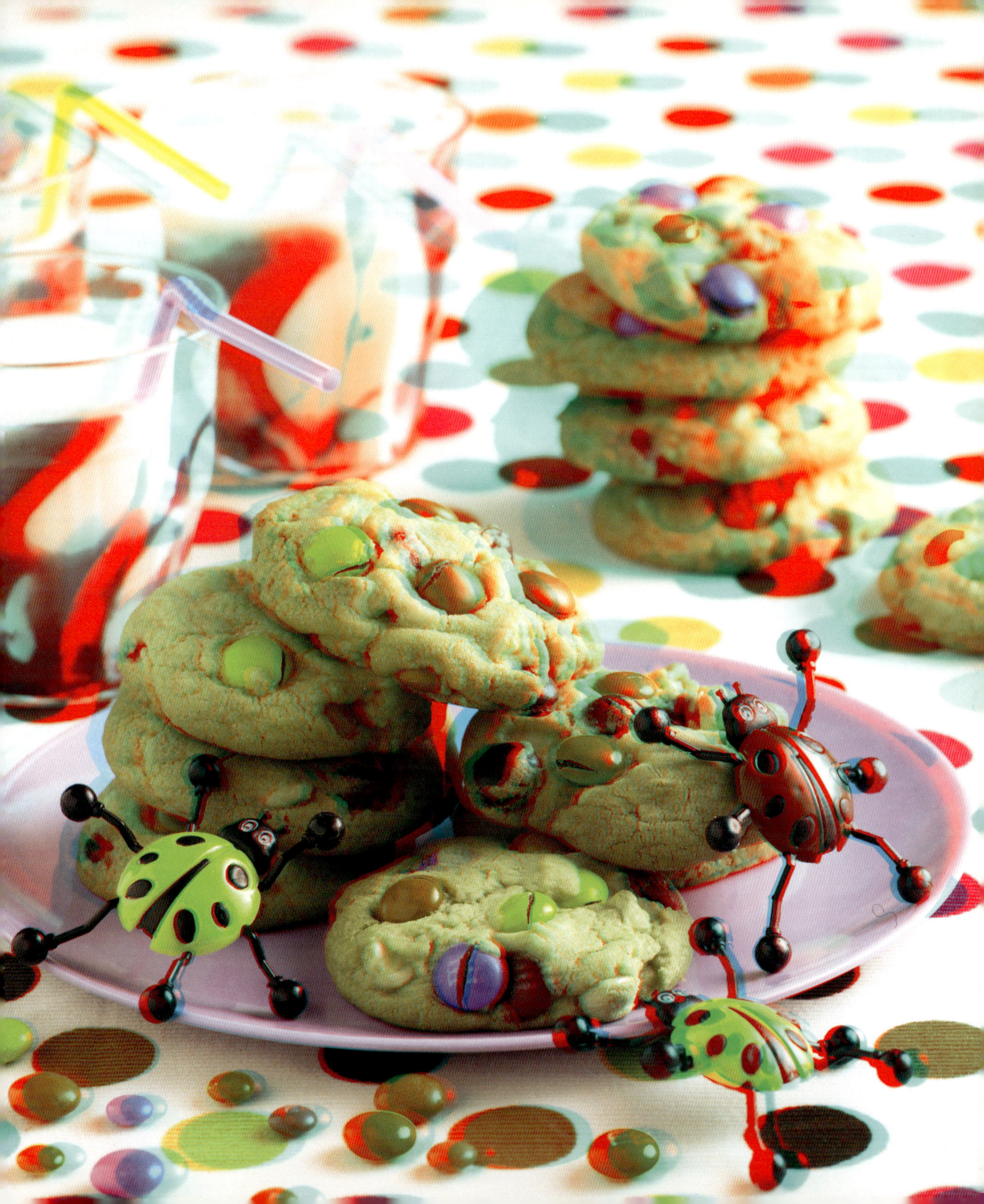

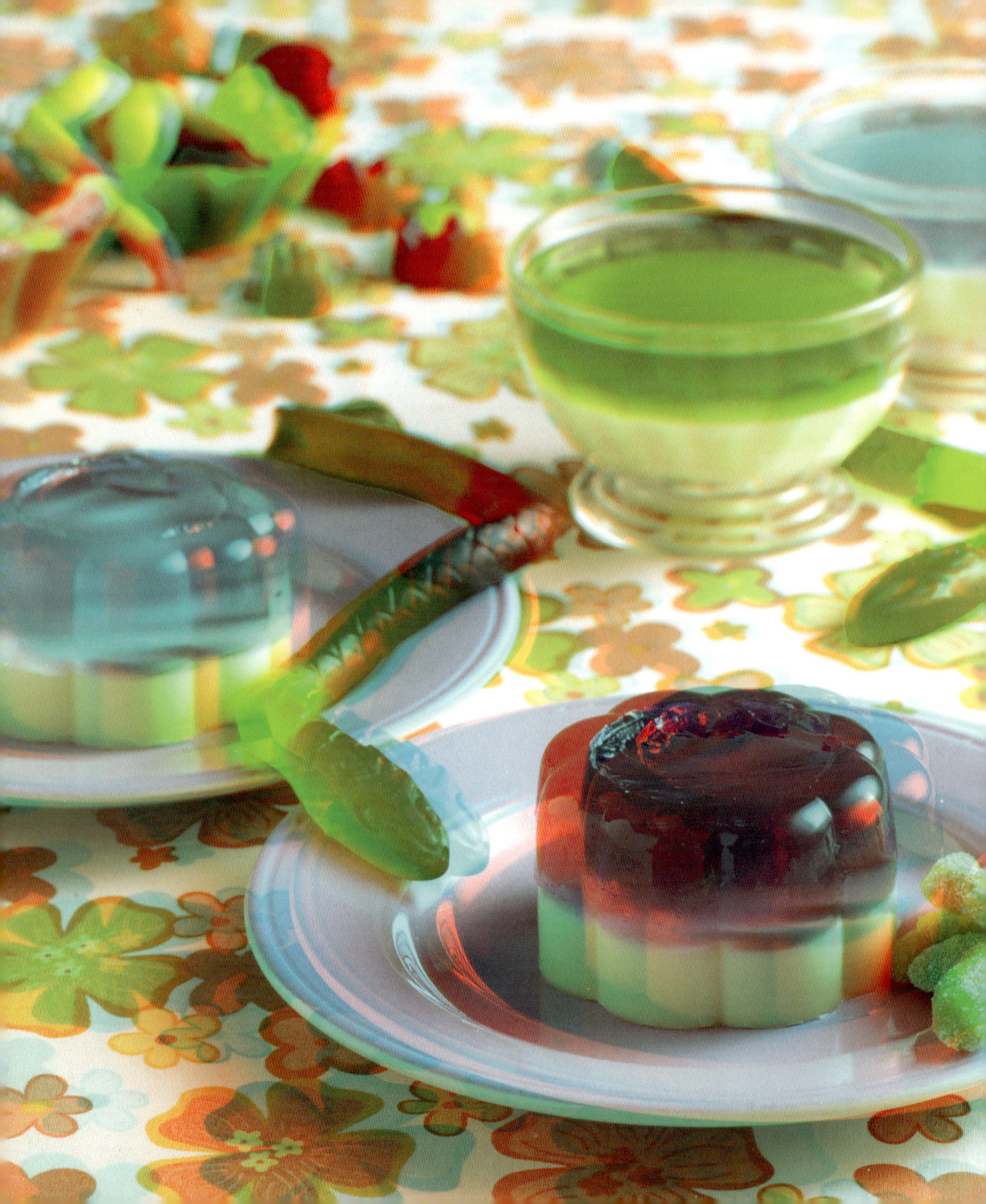

LAYERED jellies

MAKES 8 | **PREP TIME** 15 MINS | **COOKING TIME** 15 MINS

85 g (3 oz) packet **jelly crystals**
300 ml (10½ fl oz) **pouring (whipping) cream**
55 g (2 oz/¼ cup) **caster (superfine) sugar**
1 teaspoon **vanilla extract**
1½ teaspoons **gelatine**
python snakes and **sour worms**, to serve (if you like)

1. Make the jelly according to the packet directions. Divide evenly between eight 125 ml (4 fl oz/½ cup) capacity moulds or glasses (you will half fill each one). Place into the fridge for 4 hours to set.

2. Combine the cream and sugar in a small saucepan and stir over low heat to dissolve the sugar. Remove from the heat and stir in the vanilla.

3. Put 2 tablespoons cold water into a small bowl and sprinkle the gelatine over. Leave for 2 minutes, for the gelatine to soften. Stand the bowl in a larger dish of hot water and whisk with a fork to dissolve the gelatine (or microwave on high for 5 seconds).

4. Put 2 tablespoons of the cream mixture into the gelatine and stir to combine. Stir the gelatine mixture into the cream mixture. Pour into the moulds, on top of the jelly. Leave for about 3 hours.

5. To turn out of the moulds, dip into hot water for a couple of seconds, then turn onto a plate. Remove the lid if it has one. Stand for a few seconds and the jelly should slide out of the mould onto the plate.

If you are not turning out the jellies, make the cream mixture first to go in the base of the dish.

SHAGGY LAMINGTON blocks

MAKES 16 (6 LARGE & 10 SMALL) | **PREP TIME** 30 MINS | **COOKING TIME** NIL

110 g (3¾ oz/2 cups) **shredded coconut**
about 20 drops assorted **food colouring**
450 g (1 lb) ready-made **madeira (pound) cake**
250 g (9 oz/2 cups) **icing (confectioners') sugar**
about 6 drops **food colouring**, extra

1 Place the coconut into a plastic bag and add the food colouring (see note). Gently press all the air out of the bag and hold the end closed. Rub the outside of the bag, shaking occasionally to mix the colour through the coconut. Transfer to a large bowl.

2 Cut the browned top, bottom and sides off the cake and discard. Cut the cake into 3 pieces lengthways. Cut two of the pieces into 3 blocks each. Cut the other piece in half lengthways, then cut each piece into 5 smaller blocks.

3 Sift the icing sugar into a large bowl. Add 3 tablespoons hot water and extra food colouring and stir until smooth.

4 Using 2 forks, dip a piece of cake into the icing. Let the excess drip off, then place onto the coconut. Roll to coat evenly, gently pressing on the coconut. Transfer to a wire rack, handling very gently, and leave for about 30 minutes, to set.

To make different colours, divide the coconut into portions, and place into separate bags to colour. You will need to divide the icing and tint the same colour as the coconut.

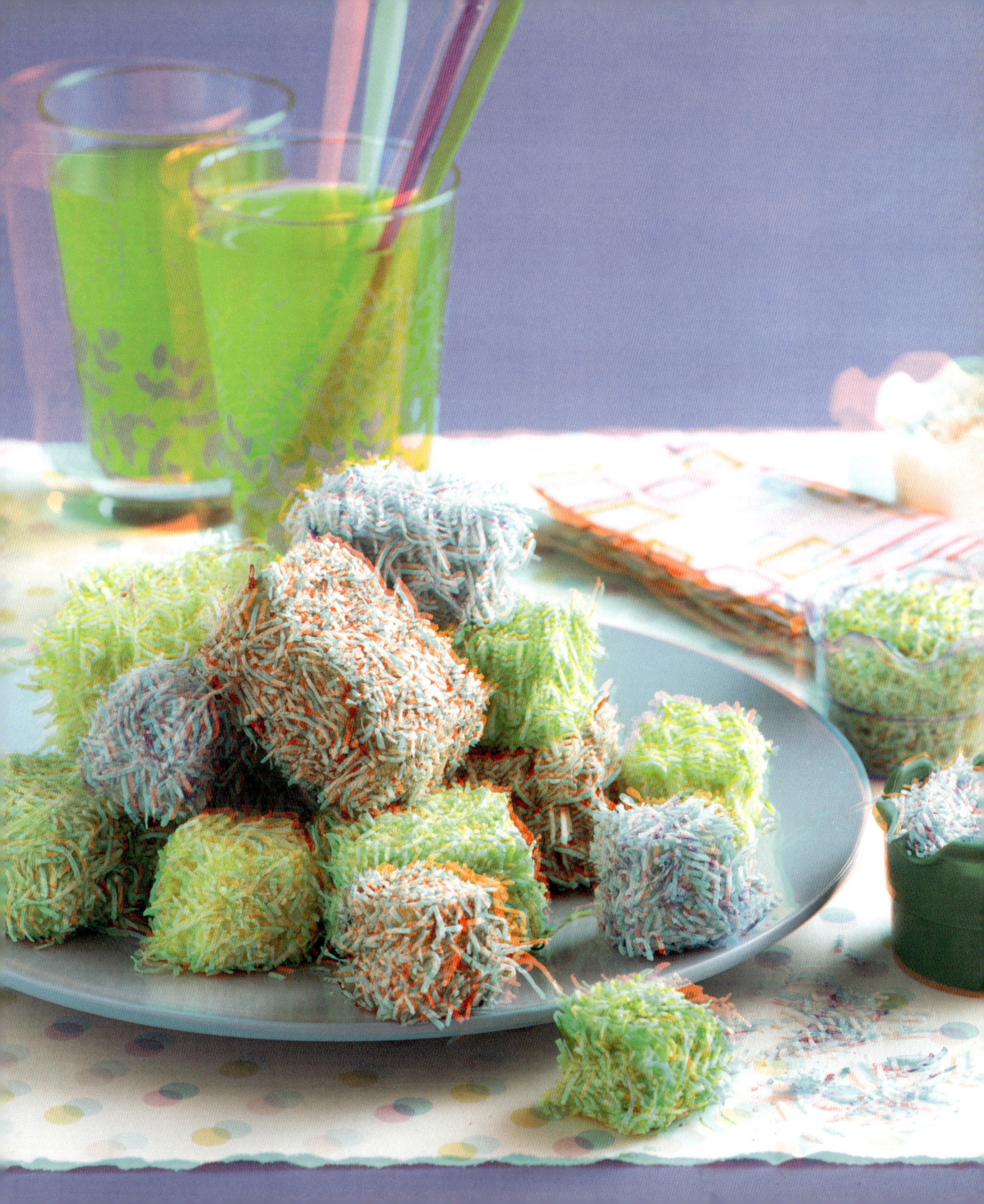

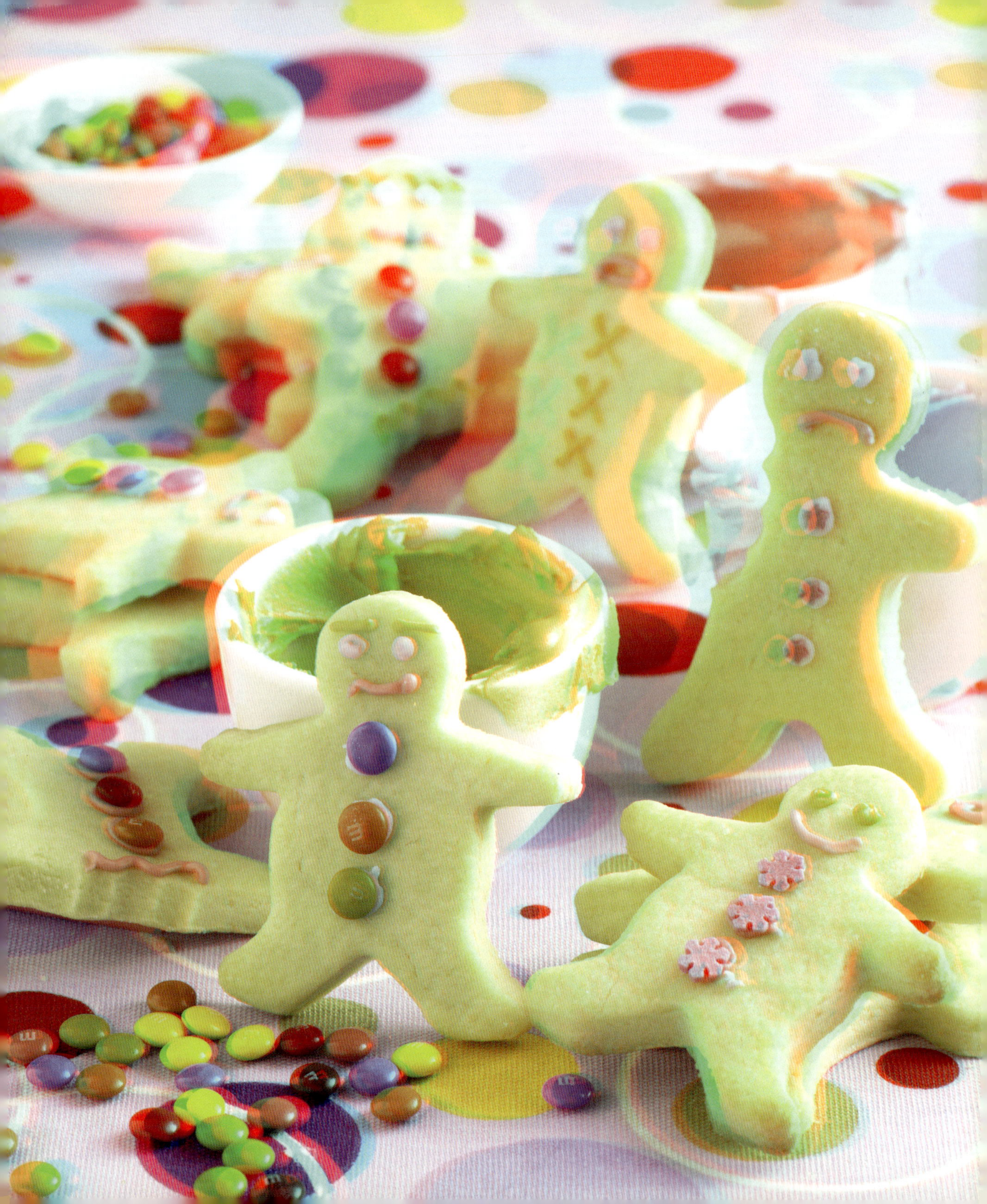

SHORTBREAD people

MAKES 16 | **PREP TIME** 12 MINS | **COOKING TIME** 40 MINS

300 g (10½ oz/2 cups) **plain (all-purpose) flour**
310 g (11 oz/2½ cup) **icing (confectioners') sugar**, sifted
200g (7 oz) **butter**, chopped
2 teaspoons **natural vanilla extract**
small **candy** and mini **m&m's**, to decorate

FROSTING
1 **egg white**
125 g (4½ oz/1 cup) **icing (confectioners') sugar**
1 teaspoon **lemon juice**
food colouring

1 Preheat the oven to 180°C (350°F/Gas 4). Line two baking trays with baking paper. Place the flour, sifted icing sugar and butter into a food processor. Process in short bursts until the mixture looks like breadcrumbs. Add 2 tablespoons cold water and process in bursts until the mixture forms small, moist clumps. Turn out onto a sheet of baking paper and gather the dough into a ball.

2 Roll out on the paper until 1 cm (½ inch) thick. Cut out shapes using cutters. Gently re-roll dough scraps and cut out more shapes. Place onto the trays. Bake for about 12 minutes, or until golden underneath (they will still be pale on top). Cool for 5 minutes on the tray, then transfer to a wire rack to cool completely.

3 To make the frosting, use a fork to whisk the egg white in a bowl until frothy. Sift the icing sugar over and add the lemon juice. Stir until smooth. Add a few drops of colouring and mix well. Put into a small piping bag fitted with a very small nozzle. Pipe faces onto the people and pipe little dots to stick candy to. Leave to set.

SUPERSTAR sundaes

MAKES 6 | **PREP TIME** 30 MINS | **COOKING TIME** ABOUT 8 MINS

350 g (12 oz/2 cups) **milk chocolate melts (buttons)**
6 large scoops **vanilla ice cream**
125 ml (4 fl oz/½ cup) **strawberry** or **caramel sauce**
mini marshmallows, choc-honeycomb bar, sprinkles, banana, wafers,
to decorate

1 Place the melts into a heatproof bowl. Place over a saucepan of simmering water and stand for 3–4 minutes, or until almost melted, then stir until smooth. Cut the zip part from 3 snap-lock sandwich bags and then cut to separate the two sides. Place a tablespoon of the melted chocolate into the centre of the plastic square. Use the back of a spoon to spread out to a neat 13 cm (5 inch) round.

2 While the chocolate is still soft, drape the piece of plastic, chocolate side up, over an upturned glass (about 5–6 cm/2–2½ inches across the base and 9 cm/3½ inches high). Repeat with the remaining chocolate to make 6 baskets. Leave for 5–10 minutes to set. Lift off the glasses and carefully peel out the plastic (try not to put your fingers all over the chocolate baskets).

3 Just before serving, scoop the ice cream into the chocolate cups. Drizzle with your choice of sauce and decorate with a selection of fruit, marshmallows and sprinkles.

Use white or dark chocolate melts if you prefer. The baskets can be made ahead of time and kept in an airtight container in the fridge.

THE KOOKY 3D KIDS' COOKBOOK

INDEX

B
bean tacos 33
beefy pies 19
biscuits, *see* cookies
buffalo chicken wings
 with creamy dip 11
burgers, chicken coleslaw 34

C
cheesy popcorn 12
chicken
 buffalo chicken wings
  with creamy dip 10
 chicken coleslaw
  burgers 34
 chunky soup with cheesy
  soldiers 42
 crunchy chicken
  fingers 29
 moneybags 23
chunky soup with cheesy
 soldiers 42
chunky spotty cookies 52
coleslaw 34
cookies
 chunky spotty cookies 52
 shortbread people 59
corn fritters 20
crispy fish nibbles with
 oven wedges 41
crunchy chicken fingers 29
cupcakes 47

D
dino pasties 16
dip, creamy 11

F
fish nibbles, crispy 41
fritters, corn 20
frosting, cupcake 47

J
jellies, layered 55

K
kebabs, lamb and vegie 30

L
lamb
 dino pasties 16
 lamb and vegie
  kebabs 30
lamington blocks, shaggy 56
layered jellies 55

M
meringue nests 48
moneybags 23

N
noodles
 san choy bau 24
 vegie and noodle
  stir-fry 38

P
pasta
 chunky soup with cheesy
  soldiers 42
 pasta with meatballs 37
pasties, dino 16
pies, beefy 19
pikelet stacks 51
pizzettes 15
popcorn, cheesy 12
pork
 pasta with meatballs 37
 san choy bau 24

S
san choy bau 24
shaggy lamington blocks 56
shortbread people 59
soup with cheesy soldiers,
 chunky 42
stir-fry, vegie and noodle 38
superstar sundaes 60

T
tacos, bean 33

V
vegie and noodle stir-fry 38

W
wedges, oven 41

Published in 2010 by Hardie Grant Books

Hardie Grant Books (Australia)
85 High Street
Prahran, Victoria 3181
www.hardiegrant.com.au

Hardie Grant Books (UK)
Second Floor, North Suite
Dudley House
Southhampton Street
London WC2E 7HF
www.hardiegrant.co.uk

Publisher: Paul McNally
Project editor: Gordana Trifunovic
Production: Penny Sanderson
Designer: Lauren Camilleri
3D imaging: Ben Hutchings
Photographer: Andre Martin
Stylist: Jane Collins
Recipe writing: Tracy Rutherford

Cataloguing-in-Publication data is available from the National Library of Australia.

ISBN 9 781 742 700 038

Printed and bound in China by 1010 Printing International Limited

Text, design & photography copyright © Hardie Grant Books 2010

All rights reserved. No part of this publication may be reproduced, stored in a retrieval system or transmitted in any form by any means, electronic, mechanical, photocopying, recording or otherwise, without the prior written permission of the publishers and copyright holders.